Contents

4

Introduction and Literature Review

1.1 Introduction

Occupational health nurses claim they "spend a great deal of their time" on "counselling". When counselling was discussed as a function of an occupational health service, at a joint meeting of the Royal Society of Medicine's Section of Occupational Medicine and the Royal College of Nursing (28 October, 1971) one person said it occupied 35% of her time. Though occupational health nurses as members of a recognized "helping" profession have reputedly always received confidences and given advice on health and other personal matters, it is only in the last decade that the term "counselling" has become widely used in this country to describe in words a function which, like many other nursing activities, had had no generally accepted term. During occupational health (O.H.) nursing training in the United Kingdom, the only preparation for this undefined, and in the early days unspecified, activity was within such topics as health education, psychology and general relationships with workers. The phrase "lending a sympathetic ear" was often used verbally to describe the activity and as recently as 1973 a German occupational health nurse described it as "massage for the soul". (Springer Organization, 1973.) Since 1973 "counselling" has been taught as a recognized part of preparation for the Royal College of Nursing O.H. Nursing Certificate. An examination of the literature reveals the development of the activity and the eventual use of the word "counselling" in occupational health nursing practice.

1.2 Literature Review

United States of America.

In the USA from whence comes the current prolific use of the word "counselling", the topic began to be studied in the later 1940s (Hoxter, 1974). The word "counselling" in their much more extensive O.H. nursing literature begins to appear at about that time. Wright (1916 and 1920) does not mention the word but describes a like activity and says that though the "entry" to the factory is in the first aid room, first aid is the least important of all O.H. nursing activities: help with "problems" is vital and it is the nurse's duty to find out why something is wrong so she can help the employee to adjust better and be "encouraged to solve his own problems". Hodgson (1933, pp. 53, 75, 95, 170) expresses a similar point of view.

Various reports such as the Public Health Nursing Section, American P.H. Association (1942) and the American Medical Association (1943) do not mention the word, but the Industrial Nursing Section* of the National Organization for Public Health Nursing (1943) and U.S. Public Health Service Bulletin 283 (1944) mentions counselling but only on health matters. In 1946 Bethel McGrath in her book "Nursing in Commerce and Industry" describes the process of counselling, the background knowledge and the appropriate attitudes inherent in good counselling, though one suspects she uses the word in the older dictionary sense of "advise/advice". She did not confine this counselling to health matters only but appreciated the wide range of topics on which employees might seek help and gave excellent descriptions of how it should be done.

As a function of O.H. nursing "counselling" begins to be mentioned with greater frequency from then on. In 1949 the American Association of Industrial Nurses in a delightfully simply written booklet says (p. 4. item 9b) that the nurse will counsel workers on all health and welfare problems of concern to them, but Wagner (1957); Henriksen (1959); Metropolitan Life (1962); Keller and May (1970) and the National Government Institute of Occupational Safety and Health (NIOSH) Hospital Occupational Health Service Study, (1975) apparently limit counselling to health matters only. However, Jane Lee (1978) in a paragraph on Health Counselling and elsewhere in her book "The New Nurse in Industry" demonstrates the wide variety of problems which will arise.

International

Internationally the word counselling was not yet in common use in O.H. nursing in 1952 when Pemberton (United Kingdom) in her report to the International Council of Nurses Nursing Service Committee, did not mention counselling or even health education as a function of O.H. nursing: papers in the joint ILO/WHO Seminar, London, 1957, do not mention the word, although the questionnaire sent to all participants asked, (Q33), "who does counselling employees on personal matters?" and several speakers described helping with employees' problems and worries.

*The term "Industrial nursing" lapsed in favour of "occupational health" after the World Health Organization used it in a Report in 1950 and the Joint ILO/WHO Seminar, London, 1957, adopted the term because "industrial nursing appears rather limited".

List of Figures

Acknowledgements

Sincere gratitude is expressed to: Professor R. S. F. Schilling, CBE, lately Professor, Occupational Health, TUC Centenary Institute of Occupational Health, London School of Hygiene and Tropical Medicine; to colleagues at the TUC Centenary Institute of Occupational Health, Dr. Paul Garton, Dr. Patrick Monard, Mr. Harry S. Shannon and Dr. Peter Taylor; to Miss Brenda Slaney of the Royal College of Nursing Institute of Advanced Nursing Education; to the Librarian of the Royal College of Nursing; to Professor Corbett McDonald of the TUCCIOH for permission to use Figures 4, 5, 6 and Table 16 and to use and adapt Figure 1; to Mrs. Gill Styman and my patient, supportive husband, Richard G. Williams and finally to the memory of Miss Irene Charley, pioneer occupational health nurse, without whose active encouragement in 1944 I should never have had the courage to venture on the long road of study and research on occupational health nursing.

Preface

Occupational health nurses have had their work and themselves studied rather less than those in other fields of nursing, so this book is of great importance. It is the beginning of understanding what occupational health nurses really do. It is not a guide to counselling, and does not offer guidance on how to do it. It does describe how the study participants say it is done and the concepts of counselling, held by these nurses, differ widely. The study concerns the amount of time spent on the activity in occupational health nursing called counselling, those who receive it and what their problems are.

The whole range of duties had to be explored to measure the time spent in counselling, and the importance attributed to it. From this it is clear that without experience and training in occupational health nursing, the nurse simply concentrates on the limited range of duties she feels confident to do, and similarly her perception of counselling is limited.

It is interesting that those who were counselled in this study were equally likely to be men or women, and that the problems dealt with in industry/commerce seemed to be similar in proportion and complexity to those found in the hospital occupational health service. There is a need for further study of the reasons for the smaller proportion of available time which could be spent in counselling in the hospital services compared to the others.

The participants agreed that they are not the only obvious counsellors in the work situation, but realised that they were in such a good position to counsel that they wished they were able to do it better. It is a pity that we have no way of knowing whether people bring their problems to occupational health nurses more nowadays than in the days when there was more informal social help in the community.

It is clear that there should be more research into what occupational health nurses do, and what influences their activities. Indeed, there are so many pointers towards future research in this study that surely they will be followed. It would be the best compliment to Mrs Williams, to whom occupational health nurses are indebted for this and her earlier work on wound dressings techniques, if they were.

DOROTHY RADWANSKI
Chief Employment Nursing Adviser
Health and Safety Executive

CHAPTER 1

Introduction and Literature Review

1.1 Introduction

Occupational health nurses claim they "spend a great deal of their time" on "counselling". When counselling was discussed as a function of an occupational health service, at a joint meeting of the Royal Society of Medicine's Section of Occupational Medicine and the Royal College of Nursing (28 October, 1971) one person said it occupied 35% of her time. Though occupational health nurses as members of a recognized "helping" profession have reputedly always received confidences and given advice on health and other personal matters, it is only in the last decade that the term "counselling" has become widely used in this country to describe in words a function which, like many other nursing activities, had had no generally accepted term. During occupational health (O.H.) nursing training in the United Kingdom, the only preparation for this undefined, and in the early days unspecified, activity was within such topics as health education, psychology and general relationships with workers. The phrase "lending a sympathetic ear" was often used verbally to describe the activity and as recently as 1973 a German occupational health nurse described it as "massage for the soul". (Springer Organization, 1973.) Since 1973 "counselling" has been taught as a recognized part of preparation for the Royal College of Nursing O.H. Nursing Certificate. An examination of the literature reveals the development of the activity and the eventual use of the word "counselling" in occupational health nursing practice.

1.2 Literature Review

United States of America.

In the USA from whence comes the current prolific use of the word "counselling", the topic began to be studied in the later 1940s (Hoxter, 1974). The word "counselling" in their much more extensive O.H. nursing literature begins to appear at about that time. Wright (1916 and 1920) does not mention the word but describes a like activity and says that though the "entry" to the factory is in the first aid room, first aid is the least important of all O.H. nursing activities: help with

13

"problems" is vital and it is the nurse's duty to find out why something is wrong so she can help the employee to adjust better and be "encouraged to solve his own problems". Hodgson (1933, pp. 53, 75, 95, 170) expresses a similar point of view.

Various reports such as the Public Health Nursing Section, American P.H. Association (1942) and the American Medical Association (1943) do not mention the word, but the Industrial Nursing Section* of the National Organization for Public Health Nursing (1943) and U.S. Public Health Service Bulletin 283 (1944) mentions counselling but only on health matters. In 1946 Bethel McGrath in her book "Nursing in Commerce and Industry" describes the process of counselling, the background knowledge and the appropriate attitudes inherent in good counselling, though one suspects she uses the word in the older dictionary sense of "advise/advice". She did not confine this counselling to health matters only but appreciated the wide range of topics on which employees might seek help and gave excellent descriptions of how it should be done.

As a function of O.H. nursing "counselling" begins to be mentioned with greater frequency from then on. In 1949 the American Association of Industrial Nurses in a delightfully simply written booklet says (p. 4. item 9b) that the nurse will counsel workers on all health and welfare problems of concern to them, but Wagner (1957); Henriksen (1959); Metropolitan Life (1962); Keller and May (1970) and the National Government Institute of Occupational Safety and Health (NIOSH) Hospital Occupational Health Service Study, (1975) apparently limit counselling to health matters only. However, Jane Lee (1978) in a paragraph on Health Counselling and elsewhere in her book "The New Nurse in Industry" demonstrates the wide variety of problems which will arise.

International

Internationally the word counselling was not yet in common use in O.H. nursing in 1952 when Pemberton (United Kingdom) in her report to the International Council of Nurses Nursing Service Committee, did not mention counselling or even health education as a function of O.H. nursing: papers in the joint ILO/WHO Seminar, London, 1957, do not mention the word, although the questionnaire sent to all participants asked, (Q33), "who does counselling employees on personal matters?" and several speakers described helping with employees' problems and worries.

*The term "Industrial nursing" lapsed in favour of "occupational health" after the World Health Organization used it in a Report in 1950 and the Joint ILO/WHO Seminar, London, 1957, adopted the term because "industrial nursing appears rather limited".

14

In Canada the Environmental Health Branch of the Ontario Department of Health, Toronto, published Margaret Hardy's (1967) report on the results of a questionnaire designed, executed and circulated by the staff of the School of Hygiene, University of Toronto, which set out to determine the functions, activities and roles of the occupational health nurse and to find out what was actually being taught to prepare nurses for occupational health nursing, though the second objective was only partially completed. The study, which produced a 50% response rate, endeavoured to define the individual tasks the nurse performed, her training or preparation for O.H. nursing work and attempted "an analysis by function of the nurse *by time*. . . to demonstrate what functions take precedence in alleviating the needs of the employed group." It appears only to be a partial record of the nurse's work, being limited to specific hours in each day, totalling 18 during a period of one week, and relied on a certain amount of estimation (see Chapter 3, Introduction). In the event, as the Report states some questions had less than 25% respond rate, and the methods used to code and process data in some areas were open to question.

> "The section which attempted to assess the adequacy of training and the individual nurse's knowledge of each of 21 activities, included counselling as an activity and defined it as "help the employee to understand himself in relation to his environment so he may be able to solve his own problems.""

but throughout the apparent assumption is that the participant would understand what "counsel" actually meant, e.g. it states "counsel on sickness absenteeism" or "provide incidental personal counselling as called for by exigencies of daily living"—the term suggests the giving of advice when coupled with such items as "provide incidental and planned counsel to employee's dietary needs and problems".

In 1968 French (United Kingdom) in a paper presented to the London meeting of the then Nursing Sub-Committee of the Permanent Commission and International Association on Occupational Health, said:

> "Counselling in its broadest sense has had an application to teaching towards (1) the protection of health and (2) the improvement in standards of health, though in its narrow sense it has come to have connotation in usage and practice in the areas of anxiety arising from difficulties of inter-personal relationships and adjustments in domestic and working environments."

The Nursing Sub-Committee (1969) in its report "The Nurse's Contribution to the Health of the worker" (English Editors), under health supervision of the individual, differentiated between health education and counselling, saying that in counselling, advice giving is avoided and the "the O.H. nurse will help the workers to arrive at their own decisions and to develop a plan that suits their individual circumstances", whilst in health education "the nurse is attempting to influence the behaviour of the worker in a particular direction". In its second report (1973) (American Editors) "The Education of the Nurse", it says the nurse's understanding and knowledge of advice, health education and counselling should be (a) principles and practices in interviewing and counselling: (b) principles and practices of learning: (c) dynamics of communication: (d) psychology of motivation and human behaviour: (e) group dynamics: and(f) concept of wellness, if she is to learn how to "counsel the employees regarding individual health program:" to which the activity is apparently limited.

Brown, (United States) in a 1969 symposium on O.H. nurse training at an ILO Occupational Safety and Health Congress in Geneva, described a course which gives instruction on counselling techniques which could be used in an occupational health mental health programme. Stoves (United Kingdom) in the same symposium, described the purpose of health counselling and its essential principles but included the statement that "counselling" could mean advice giving.

In Australia, James *et al* (1970) reporting a survey of O.H. nursing practice in the State of Victoria said:

> "a good standard of nursing care was apparent in small and medium sized firms, but in larger ones the nurse had fewer responsibilities, her potential being limited as counselling, health education and safety committee work was carried out by the medical officer when he was employed full time."

In 1973 the Health Commission of New South Wales Division of Occupational Health and Pollution Control held a week long counselling training course which offered in the programme: basic psychology, mental ill health, purpose and techniques of counselling, psychiatric treatment, counselling demonstrations, the counselling relationship, social service agencies, psychiatric services, and three practice sessions (Bundle, 1973).

By 1975 however, at the XVIII Permanent Commission Congress, the word counselling was in common use by occupational health nurses, though Yukiko Okiu's paper "Health Counselling by Occupational Health Nurses" (Japan) clearly limited it to physical health matters only. (She also told the author that the nurse would "not be allowed" to visit the factory floors in Japan.)

United Kingdom.

In the United Kingdom the only textbooks on occupational health nursing by nurses (West, 1941/49/62; Dowson-Weisskopf, 1944; Charley, 1954; Pemberton, 1965) and a doctor (Tyrer, 1961) do not mention the word but doctors Copplestone and Schilling do.

Dr. Copplestone (1967) describes both a need for the O.H. nurse to "counsel" and details how it should be done and Professor Schilling

(1973) in "Occupational Health Practice", a text book not written specifically for nurses but much used by them, describes counselling as a basic function of an O.H. Service and says it is of two sorts, one when an opportunity presents during a routine attendance and the other when the client actively seeks help, and in both instances extends beyond simple health advice. Dowson-Weisskopf (1944) refers often to "helping" and the need for the nurse to know outside agencies to which people can be referred and though health education is confined to teaching and deals mainly with personal hygiene she makes the point that the nurse must be ready "to serve all equally who have come to her for help with their hopes, fears and anxieties". West's two earlier editions talk about formal health education only but by 1962 she refers to giving individual information and advice—health education. Both Charley and Tyrer speak only of giving advice/health education, whilst Pemberton mentions neither.

As for nursing practice in the United Kingdom, by 1964 the then Royal College of Nursing (Rcn) O.H. Section (now the Rcn Society of O.H. Nursing) in its Memorandum to H.M. Government "A Hospital Occupational Health Service" included counselling as a function of such a service and in its 1968 "Implementation of a Hospital Occupational Health Service" made it quite clear that this counselling extended beyond health matters and stressed the importance of a private place for counselling to take place, without interruption and also stated that the counsellor must have a sound working knowledge of all the social agencies available. The Tunbridge Report "Care of the Health of Hospital Staff" (1968) mentioned counselling as a function of an O.H. service (paragraph 38) and describes it and the part the O.H. service plays in counselling, in detail in paragraphs 125–133.

In 1967 the newly established experimental Bedford Hospital O.H. Service in its first report included "counselling of employees" as one of their research projects and proceeded to mention counselling as an increasingly used and valuable facility in all reports up to and including the seventh and final one in 1974.

Counselling was included in the syllabus of the Rcn training programme for State Enrolled Nurses in OH nursing in 1967 while the Rcn survey of what O.H. nurse members wanted included in the preparation for the O.H. Nursing Certificate (established in 1934), reported in 1968 that nearly 50% of respondents wanted more time given to counselling. It has been included as a separate topic in O.H. Nursing preparation since 1973 and consists of an introductory course of three sessions. As a function of O.H. nursing, Rcn official O.H. information from 1964 onwards has given counselling as separate from health education and the term was freely used in O.H. nursing in 1973, as it was in all other fields—careers, education, family planning, interpersonal relationships, marriage guidance etc. The Committee on

17

Nursing (1972), commonly called the Briggs Committee, devoted no less than 24 paragraphs to counselling, what it is, why it is needed, who should do it, including the following in paragraph 593:

"Although, as we have indicated, counselling goes far wider than health matters, they have a place in a comprehensive occupational health service. In accordance with the proposals of the Joint Committee on the Care of the Health of Hospital Staff, we recommend that all nursing and midwifery staff should have access to an occupational health service. Through this occupational health service staff should also have access to a wide range of advisory services within the occupational health service to deal with the problems of greater complexity in which worries may develop into nervous or mental illness."

The National Book League (1973) produce an annotated book list of "Counselling and Guidance" for the Standing Conference for the Advancement of Counselling (SCAC) and there was a spate of study days and conferences about counselling in the nursing profession and particularly for O.H. nurses, held by the Rcn Society of Occupational Health Nursing, the Rcn Institute of Advanced Nursing Education and the Birmingham Accident Hospital Occupational Health Nurses Association. Articles on the subject appeared in the nursing press, notably Kearns (1973) and Hawkins (1973) in *Occupational Health*.

In 1975 the (draft) guidelines on O.H. Services for staff in the National Health Service said:

"Employees may consult the O.H. service in order to obtain help of a sort that can be termed as "counselling" although the specific reason for their approach to the O.H.S. may have been quite different. By "counselling" is meant the provision of personal advice, on health-related problems, which on investigation often extend into problems of relationships, career or work difficulties, and social difficulties. The provision of such a service is considered to be extremely valuable in providing O.H.S. staff with an insight into the real, as against the apparent, problems of working in the health services. O.H. services should therefore not only affect counselling facilities, but should co-ordinate the availability of other staff to undertake this function as different expertise, languages etc., may be required to gain the confidence of the clients and to understand their problems."

In 1975 Gaynor Nurse's book "Counselling and the Nurse" was published, based on and expanding her teaching to O.H. nursing and other students at the Rcn and in 1978 an Rcn Working Party published "Counselling in Nursing". Gaynor Nurse, in a personal interview with the author, (1975) said:

"the instinct and training of a nurse is to *do* something for the other person, usually actually giving personal service. Nurses also tend to feel that, as in medicine you have to get a diagnosis, do this, that and the other and the patient will get better. But in counselling this is not so."

18

She tries to get the students to see that counselling is making it possible for people to help themselves, not doing things for people, but an "enabling" process. In order to reach this goal, after the initial discussion of the students' own views, she gives them the following definition of counselling:

> "Counselling—a process through which one person helps another by purposeful conversation in an understanding atmosphere. It seeks to establish a helping relationship in which the one counselled can express his thoughts and feelings in such a way as to clarify his own situation, come to terms with some new experience, see his difficulty more objectively, and so face his problem with less anxiety and tension. Its basic purpose is to assist the individual to make his own decision from among the choices open to him." (Standing Conference for the Advancement of Counselling /SCAC/ 1969.)

Miss Nurse criticizes this only in that she dislikes the use of the word "conversation" because "so many people think it's to do with talking all the time and nowhere does it say anything about listening, but on the other hand this omission is quite useful because it can be discussed."

Development of the Use of the Word "Counselling" to describe an O.H. Nursing Activity.

It seems to the author that the trail about the activity now known as "counselling" started in O.H. nursing publications in 1916 and leads from advice and teaching about good health to a term "counselling". This term, in modern O.H. nursing practice, embraces a complex activity, (varied to meet the client's needs), which includes information, explanation, listening, clarifying, suggesting new ideas and ends with the client making up his own mind and being supported, if necessary, in carrying out his decision, with the relationship terminating when there is no longer a need for any assistance: for this activity training (and help from a peer group) is desirable.

The basis of the present concept of counselling in O.H. nursing practice has developed according partly to the social climate of the time concerning attitudes to other people. The nurse's perceived role might be said to be "education, improving, doing-good-to" in the 1920s and enabling people to develop personally and to act for themselves half a century later. The counselling activity itself has developed with the years and has been influenced by thoughts from nurses themselves about what O.H. nursing is and how they consider their various activities should be done and how performance can be improved. The search for increased effectiveness has led them to seek help from other disciplines, educationalists, psychiatrists, psychologists, social scientists and many others concerned with the present "in" word, counselling, and these influences are reflected in the way the better

19

informed O.H. nurses define the activity though some, less well informed, confine it to the 1916 version, which probably is "advice" and not "counselling" by today's high standards.

Counselling, however, is only one of many O.H. nursing activities and it needs to be seen against a background of the total work of the O.H. nurse, necessitating at least an examination of all activities to discover what proportion of all working time is spent on "counselling". The first syllabus for the O.H. Nursing Certificate course in 1934 contained all today's activities, though possibly described in other words, but over the last forty years, in the experience of the author, it is the emphasis, first more on one activity, then on another, which has continued to alter and will doubtless go on so doing. One of the results of change of emphasis has been, not necessarily an increase in the amount of counselling but in the ideas concerning it, what it is and how it should be done.

CHAPTER 2

Objectives and Methods

2.1 Objectives

Although the main purpose of this study was to examine the function of counselling by occupational health nurses, it was necessary to analyse the total workload to establish the importance of counselling in relation to all the other O.H. nursing functions, through almost any one of which the opportunity of counselling could arise. The study aimed to determine:

1. The proportion of the nurses' time which was spent in counselling;
2. The nurses' own opinions about what counselling is;
3. Who were the persons who were counselled and the type of problems dealt with;
4. To record the training and O.H. experience of the nurses; to see if these influenced how much and what sort of counselling was done.

2.2 Methods

The TUCCIOH Study

The TUC Centenary Institute of Occupational Health (TUCCIOH), London School of Hygiene and Tropical Medicine, University of London, surveyed Hospital Group occupational health services in the National Health Service on behalf of H.M. Government's Department of Health and Social Security. The author was a member of the TUCCIOH team and as one of her particular assignments, analysed all nursing activites during time spent at work and also made a detailed study of counselling. Out of this work the present extended study on counselling developed. Consequently some of the methods and the services included in the study were determined upon because it was part of the much larger survey. The study of the hospital O.H. services was extended to include services in industry and commerce, so that finally the work of nurses in O.H. services in eleven hospitals and six industrial/commercial undertakings was studied.

Selection

Hospital Services

For the TUCCIOH survey, in 1971 a questionnaire was sent to the 332 hospital groups* in England and Wales. The 329 replies indicated that only 35 hospital groups had an O.H. service. The decisive criteria were that these services *claimed* to offer more than just treatment and medical examination, they also claimed to put "some emphasis on selecting the right person for the right job at interview or medical examination, monitoring the working environment, possibly doing some research into the cause of sickness absence, accidents and labour turnover." (Monard *et al,* 1974)

The hospital services eventually studied were partly self-selected because these 35 hospital groups were approached and asked to participate in a very much more detailed study, but after examination of the very considerable amount of work for the whole study, which involved most departments in each hospital, only fourteen finally agreed. It is believed the main reason for refusal was the extra work. Of these fourteen, three could not do an activity analysis, (one suspects reluctance to have an inadequate service closely examined) so that the author's study concerns eleven hospitals: four acute urban (codes ABEK), three acute rural (FGH), three acute metropolitan (CDJ) and one psychiatric rural (I).

Industrial/Commercial Services

For the industrial/commercial group a published appeal (*Occupational Health, 1973*) and verbal requests at several occupational health nursing meetings resulted in only one definite offer: so help was directly sought from five more enterprises (none refused), selected to give typical examples of different types of industry and commerce:

Unit 1.	A public utility undertaking.
Units 2 & 3.	Precision assembly/office work.
Unit 4.	Heavy engineering/foundry.
Unit 5.	Manufacturing, with high trauma hazard.
Unit 6.	Scientific research and development.

Recording

Recording was done by the participants on charts or forms. Definitions of counselling were noted and recorded on tape during personal interviews, as were N.H.S. nursing establishment grades

*The then hospital groups were comprised of one to six hospitals, depending on size and location.

(where applicable), O.H. nursing qualifications and O.H. experience, and the "age" of the service.

Activity Analysis Recording.

O.H. services have a certain amount of choice in the priorities given to certain aspects of their work, but a *case load record* alone indicates only part of the work actually performed and not the amount of time spent on each different function or activity.

Four practicable methods of analysis were examined:

(a) *Independent observers* recording all activities and duration thereof. This was impossible because it was too expensive and because some modification of behaviour is inevitable.

(b) *Keeping a written diary.* This had been tried in 1972 (Monard *et al*, 1974) in the Bedford Hospital Occupational Health Service, but it was found to be very time consuming, onerous in decision making (i.e. how to decide which activity was being performed at any one time) and difficult to classify into usable results.

(c) *A tape-recorded diary.* This had also been tried by the Bedford Hospital O.H. Service, and had the same drawbacks as the written diary, with the added problems of obtaining reliable transcription.

(d) *An activity analysis chart.* This was the method chosen as it seemed to offer the best way of getting accurate data on the work of the nurse with as little inconvenience and disturbance of normal work as possible. Although, as with other methods, there would be inaccuracies, it was considered likely that these would not significantly affect results.

Chart Development

A chart (Figure 1) was designed by the author and was printed so that three sheets covered a period of 12 hours (8 a.m. to 8 p.m.) but also permitted adaptation to cover work between 8 p.m. and 8 a.m. where necessary. The unit of time selected was five minutes, based on findings by Altschul (1964) that this was the most convenient unit when nurse tutors were recording how they spent their time.

Pilot Study

The chart was tested for a period of one week in six O.H. services—three hospitals, a food factory, a heavy engineering factory and a Government Research & Development Establishment. It was found to be a practicable method but at the participants' recommendation, overall size of the sheets was made larger—actually $13'' \times 16\frac{1}{2}''$ wide—

Activity Chart

Figure 1.

x shows span
x = five minutes or less   x | of an
x   activity

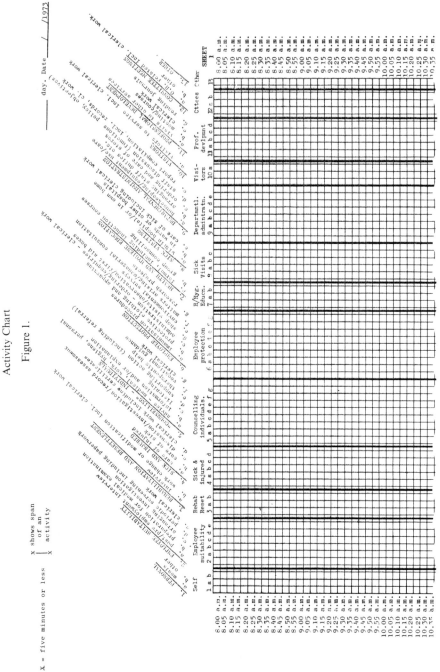

© TUC Centenary Institute of Occupational Health

24

a smaller size being "too fiddley". The charts were printed with columns for the thirteen main headings across the top, each column sub-divided and with an explanation of these sub-divisions above, and the times of the day down each side. Time spent on an activity was recorded by placing a cross in the square for the starting and finishing times and then joining the two vertically. If two activities were done at once, both were recorded.

List of Activities

The Activities were:
1. *Personal.* a. meals; b. other.
2. *Employee suitability* a. post/pre employment interview; b. preparation for medical examination; c. arranging investigation; d. periodic screening including paperwork; c. clerical work.
3. *Rehabilitation and resettlement.* a. interview; b. work change and modification including clerical work.
4. *Sick and injured.* a. care of injured; b. care of sick; c. discussion/investigation/record assessment; d. clerical work including certificates.
5. *"Counselling" individuals.* a. advice—medical, work, hygiene, personal; b. information and/or explanation; c. listening; d. supporting action (including referral); e. therapeutic help; f. vocational guidance; g. clerical work.
6. *Employee protection* a. immunization procedures; b. protective clothing and apparatus; c. administration—observations/first aid boxes; e. environmental surveys; f. matters arising/managerial consultation; g. research projects.
7. *Health and hygiene education.* a. formal, including induction courses; b. group counselling.
8. *Sick visiting.* a. within hospital/or in own home; b. in wards or other hospitals; c. care of sick including clerical work.
9. *Departmental administration.* a. housekeeping/equipment use/care; b. arranging staff duties etc; c. ordering and care of stores; d. staff discussion (functions, policy, objectives); e. report compilation, including records, clerical work.
10. *Visitors.* a. visitors to service including clerical work.
11. *Professional development.* a. visits to other services; b. meeting/courses; c. clerical work; d. reading journals.
12. *Committee meetings.* a. O.H. related, including clerical work; b. other.
13. *G.P. work* (and not "other" as printed on the sheet, see below.)
14. *Other.*

Following discussions with the hospital participants when the charts and instructions were distributed, it was decided to designate activity column 13 as "assistance to doctors performing G.P. services" as so many performed this activity because the O.H. doctor was frequently the G.P. for resident staff, something which did not apply to the I/C group. Any unclassified activity such as attending hospital or other functions, chiropody clinics etc., were recorded as such under column 14. It was made clear to participants that this document did not suggest they should be doing all of the listed activities.

Distribution

Supplies of charts, sufficient to cover more than 20 days work for each nurse and, where there was one, the secretary (since clerical staff relieve the nurse of work she would otherwise have to do), were delivered by the author personally, their completion demonstrated and a written explanation (Figure 2) also left with them. Recording was for four consecutive weeks, i.e. 20 days work, which was what was analysed. Some services continued for a longer period from choice, whilst one hospital (D) was able to complete it only for one day, but completed all other records.

Calculation/Analysis

The total times each person spent on the main activities and their subdivisions were added together and agreed with the total time at work. If two activities were recorded simultaneously the time was divided proportionately but another activity during a meal time resulted in deletion of the personal time for that particular period. For ease of counting it would have been better if the time of day had been printed against a line instead of against a square space (=five mins.) but both lead to difficulty. A transparent straight edge, calibrated to match the five minute squares, held against the vertical connecting lines drawn by the participants expedited counting, because the length of time could be read at a glance.
From these sheets it was possible to calculate:

1. The proportion of time spent on each activity by each individual participant during the time at work.
2. Counselling time as a percentage of all work done.
3. The total proportion of time spent in direct personal contact i.e. face-to-face with a patient.
4. Counselling time as a percentage of personal patient contact.
5. The proportion of time spent on clerical work.
6. The clerical work involved in counselling, or various other items.

26

Figure 2.

O.H. Survey. Nursing Service Activity Analysis.
(Letter left with *each* participant, bearing the address and telephone number of the research worker.)

This chart is divided into five minute intervals for each day for recording the various activities of an occupational health nursing service. Three sheets of paper are needed per day—morning, afternoon and evening—and each sheet should bear the date and the code number. Eventually each column will be totalled and each activity shown as a percentage of the entire day. If time is spent in the department or in the work place between 8 p.m. and 8 a.m., the word "night" should be written against the time scale, thus for the period 8 p.m. onwards, the morning time sheet should be used. If work is done at home (often done to avoid interruptions) this should be shown by writing the time taken on the task on the last sheet of the day, e.g. "at home 8 p.m. to 10 p.m. annual report."

The time spent on any activity should be indicated by a cross for five minutes or less—longer on any one activity by joining two marks by a vertical line. If, during the course of any main activity you are interrupted for more than five minutes record it but do not leave this time out of your main activity recording. This particularly applies to your own meal times which if spent "working" should show double recording lines.

"13. other"

If a nurse is occupied for a period attending a G.P. who is holding a G.P. List clinic ("branch surgery") this should be entered under column 13 and marked G.P. list. But if she is occupied attending a G.P. who is holding an occupational health clinic for sick and injured, even if a few of the patients *happen* to be on his own G.P. list, this should be entered under 4.

A nurse may be occupied with some activity which cannot be classified under any of the headings—in this case please enter it under 14, but please specify the activity.

Some people may feel that at certain times of pressure they cannot analyse their activities in the detail shown. In this case please record time spent under the number of the activity, not the letters, but it would be greatly appreciated if the counselling column could be completed in detail, where possible.

If there are any queries, please do not hesitate to telephone me. If out, I can always call you back!

(signed) M. Margaret Williams.

Having calculated these details for an individual participant, it was possible to combine them for the whole O.H. service, whether it was provided for one nurse or several, and to combine services together.

2.3   Classification of Patients' Problems Brought for Counselling.

The Table of Classifications

The classification of problems dealt with, was developed after questioning a large number of O.H. nurses. There are 22 classifications, under four main headings: A. Health; B. Problems of Personal Relationships; C. Career or Work Problems; D. Social Problems. Problems concerning personal relationships, B.5. family, has a further five sub-divisions and so did B.6. sex. It will be seen from Figure 3 that these classifications are simply worded and in use apparently posed no particular difficulties to participants. A copy of the complete list of classifications was left with each participant, together with a written explanation, which was also given verbally by the author. (Figure 3)

Classification A.1. (health problems/self) was included because some called this "consultation" and others "counselling" a semantic distinction probably connected with a traditional reluctance to presume to use a word usually associated with another discipline.

Recording

For another purpose concerning the TUCCIOH study, the *hospital O.H. nurses* were recording each attendance and what it was for, on specially designed forms (Figure 4). If the item of service was entered as "counselling", the O.H. nurses added a letter and number to indicate which of the four main types of problems, and any relevant sub-division, was the one concerned: if there was more than one problem at any one time, these were indicated in order of apparent importance to the client. For example, A1, B5(b), D,1,2, 5 would mean—Health/self: personal relationships/family/children: social/money/living accommodation/race relations.

N.B. The industrial/commercial group nurses did not complete this form for *every* patient dealt with, but only when counselling was given, see below.

The problems classified by the hospital services were then recorded on punched feature cards (Jolley, 1968). Information was studied (for the hospital services) for approximately the same 20 days out of a three month recording—the number of cases varied very little month by month. The period was the same as for the activity analysis record in each case.

28

Figure 3

Table of Classifications

A. HEALTH PROBLEMS
1. Concerning self, including straight information answering a question like "I have a corn what should I do?"
2. Of relatives
3. Of friends
4. Other employees

B. PROBLEMS OF PERSONAL RELATIONSHIPS
1. Colleagues at same level
2. Client's "manager"
3. Client's own staff
4. Other employees

5. Family	(a)	Parents	(d)	Sibling
	(b)	Children	(e)	Other relatives
	(c)	Spouse		
6. Sex	(a)	Spouse	(d)	Family Planning
	(b)	Male Friend	(e)	Self
	(c)	Female Friend		

7. Other

C. CAREER OR WORK PROBLEMS
1. Own professional development including study difficulties
2. Need for support in carrying out own job
3. Stress/frustration in own work
4. Future career/discussion—vocational guidance
5. Other

D. SOCIAL PROBLEMS
1. Money
2. Living accommodation
3. Travel difficulties
4. Redundancy/Retirement
5. Race relations
6. Other

Classification of Counselling Problems.

If "counselling" is checked on the nurses' attendance daily sheets*, please (a) indicate M. or S. instead of the usual mark, to tell us the marital state of the patient. For this purpose, divorced, separated, widowed persons should be classified as married.** (b) put the classification of the problem in the last four columns, using as much space as is necessary, since you may deal with more than one problem in the course of one counselling. (e.g. A1: B5(b): D1, 2, 5.)

*Figures 4 and 5. **See page 32, 2.4.

Figure 4

Date: ....   Sheet No. ....

Staff categories: 1. Medical and dental
                    2. Trained nurses and midwives
                    3. Nurses and midwives in training
                    4. Auxiliary nurses
                    5. Professional and Technical
                    6. Administrative and Clerical
                    7. Works, Maintenance and Domestic

* Separate register of findings requiring further action.

* Name not required by study team.

Department or Name*	Staff Category	M	F	Resident	Non Resi

NURSES DAILY ATTENDANCE SHEET

dent	Pre-employment Interview (P = passed, F = failed)	Post employment Interview (P = passed, F = failed)	Periodic screening examination (P = passed, F = failed)	Referred to doctor for investigation	Routine investigation for investigation (P = passed, F=failed)	Immunisation procedure ordered*	Return after sickness absence interview	Further action taken on above	Consultation	Special Investigation	Treatment	Treatment at request of doctor	Initial treatment of injury	Subsequent treatment of injury	Septic wounds	Referral to O.H.M.O./G.P./Consultant	Preparation for medical exam. (Urinalysis, B.P. etc.)	Counselling	Formal hygiene talk (Department)	Environmental visit

Note on Figure 4

These sheets, (Figure 4) related to another part of the TUCCIOH Survey and were completed only by hospital services. To save expense, some of the same forms, but modified, were utilized for the industrial/commercial group.

Using the same but modified forms, the *industrial/commercial* group also recorded problems in the same way as the hospital group, also during the same 20 days as the activity analysis. Because this group was not using the forms for any other purpose a "cover" was provided to fit the top of the form (Figure 4) so that all that could be read were the headings "Department or name", "Staff category", "M/F" and columns in which to write the problem classification(s). As will be seen from Figure 5 the "cover" also contained the instructions for recording and classification, as a reminder of what had been explained by the author. The data were analysed and calculated by hand because the quantity did not warrant the expense of punched card analysis. A check was made to ensure accuracy of transfer of recordings.

Figure 5. Modified Figure 4 for Industrial/Commercial Group

* Name not required by study team.

Department or Name*	Staff Category	M	F																		

Pretend that each sheet has on it only what is now showing on this sheet.

During or at the end of the day, as is convenient, though it is best at the time, go through your daily attendance records for your own cases and then write down a works or attendance number or name (so you know the one you've entered if you are interrupted) and write whether the client's staff category is weekly/monthly or whatever gradings you use to differentiate different types of workers, tick for male or female and then decide the classification of the problems about which you counselled him or her. If there was more than one problem put them down too, say A2, B6c, D1, etc. If the problem does not come under a given classification give the 'other' number and if you can, say what the problem is.

Analysis

The numbers recorded for each classification were then noted for each participant and service within both hospital and industrial/commercial groups and for both groups together.

2.4 Staff Use of Counselling Services

Recording

In the *hospital* O.H. services the national Health Service (N.H.S.) employment category, sex, whether resident or non-resident, were

Figure 6.

Structured Interview Form Used for Line Managers in Hospitals. (Monard *et al,* 1974. App. 6:)

1.	Have you had any contact with the occupational health service in your hospital?	Yes/No
2.*	Has the service ever been a help, in any way, (a) to you as a manager or (b) to any members of your department?	(a) Yes/No (b) Yes/No
3.*	Do you know what services for staff the occupational health service offers?	Yes/No
4.	Are there any special risks in the work done in your department?	Yes/No
	If "yes" please specify	
	. . . .	
5.*	Does the occupational health service know about these risks?	Yes/No
6.*	Has the occupational health service helped you to do anything about them?	Yes/No
7.	Can you suggest ways in which the service could be improved? (Please speak freely, your suggestions will be absolutely confidential.)	
	. . . .	
	. . . .	
8.*	Would you say the contribution of the occupational health service to the health and welfare of hospital staff was:	

a. very valuable   b. valuable

c. of little value   d. valueless

(The one most nearly representing the opinion is to be ticked.)

9.   If "c" or "d" to question 8, please explain why you think so . . . .

. . . .

10.   Do you think an occupational health service should be introduced in every hospital in the country?

Yes   Qualified   No

11.   Why do you say that? . . . .

. . . .

* questions used for assessment rating.

SCORING. Positive answers to questions 2a, 2b, 3, 5 and 6 were allocated one point each and question 8 offered a chance of scoring 3, 2, 1 or 0 points.

$$\text{Equation} = \frac{\text{points scored} \times 100}{8 \times \text{number of respondents.}}$$

(Interview numbers varied between hospitals)

recorded for each attendance, using the same form as the the problem classification record. For the *industrial/commercial* group, again this was done but only where the attendance involved counselling and as there were no staff categories comparable with those in the N.H.S. a simple grouping into weekly and monthly paid staff was adopted ("works" and "staff"): none was resident. All the other information was identical in both groups. The proportion of men to women in the total work force in each industrial/commercial undertaking was established. Both groups found it difficult and liable to cause offence if marital status was recorded and the attempt to establish this was therefore abandoned.

Analysis

Again for the hospital service, the data were put on to punched feature cards (Jolley 1968) and the industrial/commercial services data analysed by hand.

2.5 Nurses' Definition of Counselling

Recording and Analysis

The author interviewed each senior (sometimes the only) O.H. nurse in each service in the hospital and the industrial/commercial groups in order to get their definitions of counselling. Tape recordings were made of their answers to the questions "Do you do any counselling?" and "What do you mean by this term?". Replies were transcribed and analysed. At the same interview their staff grade in the "Salmon" nursing structure (which only operates in N.H.S. hospitals) and for all of them, their O.H. training and O.H. experience were recorded, and also how long the service had been established. The information was then tabulated.

2.6 "Quality" of the Hospital O.H. Services

As part of the TUCCIOH Survey Dr. Paul Garton and the author had made a *subjective assessment* of high, medium or low for each hospital service, based on information obtained and personal observations. Also, by means of a structured interview with departmental managers, a quality rating for each hospital O.H. service was obtained. The questions asked and the method of scoring are given in Figure 6: scores above 85% were rated "high", between 84% and 65% "medium" and 64% and below, "low". These findings (Monard *et al*, 1974) were used by the author in attempting to estimate the influence of training and O.H. experience on counselling work done by O.H. nurses.

CHAPTER 3

Results and Discussion

Section I

3.1 Introduction

Although various studies have been undertaken by the Society of Occupational Health Nursing (Royal College of Nursing) which established the functions of an occupational health nurse, there appears to be no published work concerning the amount of time spent on each of the tasks performed by O.H nurses in the United Kingdom. Some Chief or Principal Nursing Officers of large enterprises have reported unpublished studies of work done in their own O.H. nursing services, but no detailed recordings of all time spent at work, though some estimates have been made. Estimates are not always reliable. For example, Monard *et al.* (1974) reported that nurses in hospital O.H. services were asked to estimate the number of hours per week spent on clerical work, and these were then given as a percentage of their total working hours. When the same services recorded their activities, the lowest underestimation was 4% and the highest 30%, the actual percentage of time being very much higher in every instance. In the same study, there was also a similar underestimate, by administrative officers, of labour turnover when the estimates were compared with actual figures.

The Canadian study of the work of O.H nurses in Ontario (M. Hardy, 1967) which obtained only part of the information sought, is unsuitable for comparison with the present study, not only because many of the figures are estimates but also the survey dealt with only part of a working day and week. (see page 15).

3.2 Methods

Activity Analysis—General

For a period of 20 working days nurses' work in seventeen Occupational Health Services was recorded, totalling some 4,730 hours, undertaken by 39 people. Eighteen full-time and 12 part-time occupational health nurses, one full-time and eight part-time clerks participated.

This present study of only 17 O.H. services represents the work done by O.H. nurses in a very small proportion of all O.H. services in the

U.K. and might, therefore, be considered to be too small but this was unavoidable. Although the common limitations of time and money obtained, what really restricted the size of the study as far as *hospital groups* were concerned was that, at that time, so very few services were in existence, only 35 in 329 Hospital Management Committee Groups. (Until the 1974 reorganization of the NHS, a hospital management committee group consisted of between one and six hospitals, depending on size and location.) Also the study was part of a much larger one on these same services. Participation could not be compulsory and agreement depended not only on the co-operation of O.H. service staff but on many other departments, all of whom were required to do a great deal of extra work for the main study, with the result that only 11 hospital groups were studied.

The industrial/commercial services were not a random sample since all were volunteers and partly self-selected in that they agreed to help when approached—none refused—but they were asked as representing various types of general industry and commerce, were varied in size and located in differing parts of England, as were the hospitals. The author had no detailed knowledge of any of these services before the study commenced, just that the organization had an O.H. service.

Nevertheless the overall results are so close between the two groups of services that it is believed that these fairly describe their work and probably also give a reasonable picture of the work of O.H. nurses in the U.K.

The methods used to *collect information* were simple and most of the participants said they enjoyed the exercise, which seems to indicate that both the chart for the activity analysis and the forms for recording the classification of problems and staff counselled, were reasonably good ways of obtaining the information.

The list of *classification of problems* was based on the personal experience of the author together with suggestions made during much discussion with colleagues. The terminology was deliberately simple. An Officer of the then Race Relations Board, at a 1974 SCAC Conference in Rugby, was concerned because he had had a list of problems presented to him by a psychiatrist who had acted as Counsellor to the Officer's own staff and the groups of the various types of problems appeared to be very different. When closely compared, however, what emerged was that the lists were remarkably similar, it was just that the psychiatrist had used technical phrases whereas the author had used a simpler terminology.

3.3 The Activity Analysis

Time on Each Activity

As has already been explained, (Chapter 2), it was necessary to examine the total function of the O.H. nursing services and the proportion of time spent on each activity through a full activity analysis, in order to obtain the desired information about counselling. Full details of these results are given and discussed in Appendix 1, but it must be emphasized that these should not be taken to imply that results indicate ideal allocations of time, since the work of any service is subject to so many variations, according to the way a service is run, organization of time being largely determined by how the doctor and nurse perceive their function. The allocation is also affected by the employers wishes, the policy of the company or management committee, or the terms of reference suggested by the employer, many of whom have very narrow concepts of what an O.H. service should do, though experienced practitioners of good occupational health usually manage to overcome these limitations. The inexperienced tend to give only a limited service. The correct proportion of working time devoted to each (or any new) O.H. nursing activity also depends on the needs of the working group and the skill and ability of practitioners to perceive and meet the needs. Certain faults are revealed in this study, such as the fact that almost no attention is paid to some important aspects, such as rehabilitation and resettlement and, in the case of the hospitals, to employee protection other than immunization.

Table 1 shows the percentage of all time worked spent on each activity:

1. by services in the hospital group: Column I;
2. by services in the industrial/commercial group: Column II;
3. by both together: Column III;
4. the ratings for the activities, most to least: Column IV

From this latter it will be seen that Counselling, 5% of all time worked, rated seventh in importance, but it also shows that the rating differs very little between the two groups.

Differences between Groups

Nevertheless there were *differences in practice* between the hospital and the industrial/commercial services, the *greatest being* in the amount of time spent on *employment suitability,* Activity 2. The hospital group's 28% is more than twice as much as the industrial/commercial group's 13%, but this difference is because the hospital services spend so much time on clerical work for this activity. Indeed this is true in all their activities. (see Appendix I).

The next *largest difference* in practice between the two groups is in *counselling,* Activity 5, where the industrial/commercial group do almost twice as much as the hospitals (7%/4%), though the difference is insignificant as a percentage of all time worked, but not of direct patient contact. (Table 2).

TABLE 1

Activity analysis for hospital group, industry/commerce group and for both groups combined, with ratings (= % activity as % of all time worked).

Activity	I Hospitals	II Ind./commerce	III Both	IV Ratings I	II	III
1. Personal*	10	12	11	6	5	5
2. Empl. suitability	28	13	23	1	3	1
3. Rehab./Restl.	0.8	2	1	9	8	9
4. Sick/injured	16	26	19	2	1	2
5. Counselling	4	7	5	7	6	7
6. Empl. protection**	11	13	12	5	3	4
7. Hlth. Hyg. Ed.	0.6	1	0.8	10	10	10
8. Sick visits	2	2	2	8	8	8
9. Dept. Admin.	15	17	16	3	2	3
10. 'Other' total***	12	7	11	4	6	5
Total hours studied	3,110	1,619	4,729 hrs. 45 mins.			
No. staff FT/PT	19/9	7/4	26/13			

*includes meals.

**immunization, protective clothing, shop visits, environmental surveys, managerial consultation.

***includes visitors, professional development, committees, G.P. work, 'other'.

38

The general conclusion concerning how O.H. nurses spent their time is that the better services in both the hospital and industrial/commercial groups spread their time fairly well over all the activities, the exact proportion varying according to their situation and expertise. (See Appendix I). On the whole, the industrial/commercial group spreads its time more evenly over all the activities than the hospital group. This spread is desirable, since an O.H. service should cover all activities, though sick visits (Activity 8) should occupy very little, if any, occupational health time. It is as bad for an O.H. nurse to spend all her time tying up cut fingers without finding out why they are cut and remedying this through management, as it is to do "medicals" but not know the physical, mental and emotional parameters of the job the person is going to do or the conditions under which it will be done. The purpose of an O.H. medical is to see if the person is fit to do that job, though it is also useful to record the existing state of health.

Time on Personal Contact with "a" Patient

Though all occupational health is concerned with people and their working conditions, some of the time the nurse is face to face with an individual (i.e. directly with patients or in personal contact with 'a' patient) or on activities concerned with or about 'a' patient and it is during these periods that counselling takes place.

TABLE 2

Hospitals: Industrial/Commercial: Both:

Time spent on or about patients as % of all time worked.

Detail	Hospitals	Ind./Comm.	Both
I. All time on or about 'a' patient, i.e. Acts. 2 to 6.	59%	61%	60%
II. Acts 2–6, as in A above less clerical work.	37%	51%	43%
III. Acts 2–6, direct personal contact with 'a' patient, not 'about' a patient.	29%	33%	30%
IV. Clerical work of Acts. 2–6.	63%	49%	58%

Table 2 shows that the industrial/commercial group spent a higher proportion of time directly with patients than the hospital group, whether it is in the total of activities 2–6, i.e. all activities concerned with or about 'a' patient, e.g. including making enquiries, contacting a supervisor or another agency etc. (Part I) or activities 2–6 with the clerical content deducted (Part II) or in direct, personal face-to-face contact with 'a' patient and excluding clerical work and actions about 'a' patient (Part III). The hospital group spent 29% of time directly in contact with patients, the industrial/commercial group 33% and both as one group, 30% on this. These differences are not significant but the differences in clerical work was—hospitals 63% on clerical work about 'a' patient, industrial/commercial group, 49%. (Part IV). (See also Appendix I).

3.4 Time on Counselling

Table 3 gives details of counselling and shows that the

TABLE 3

Counselling. Activity 5.

Detail	Hospitals	Ind./Comm.	Both
I. Total activity connected with counselling as % of all time worked.	3.7%	7%	4.8%
II. Counselling as % of time spent on or 'about' a patient, i.e. Acts. 2–6.	6.2%	11.5%	8.0%
III. Counselling (less clerical as % of time in direct personal contact with patient (i.e. not 'about' or clerking).	10.5%	19.9%	14.15%
IV. Clerical work as % of the total counselling activity.	16.0%	2.5%	9.3%

industrial/commercial group spent almost twice as much time on it as the hospital group, whether it is calculated as:

   I. Counselling as a percentage of *all time worked.*

  II. Counselling as a percentage, of all time worked, *on or about "a" patient.*

 III. Counselling as a percentage of all time in *direct personal contact* with 'a' patient.

 IV. This part of Table 3 again confirms that the hospital group spent much more time on clerical work than the industrial/commercial group for this activity, 16% compared with 2.5%.

Table 4 gives details of counselling as a percentage of *all time worked* by the individual services composing the two groups, i.e. greater detail for Part I of Table 3, the total activities connected with counselling as a percentage of all time worked, (from Appendix 1).

TABLE 4

Detail of time spent on counselling as a % of all time worked. Part I, Table 3.

Hospitals	Industry/commerce	Both
A – 3% B – 4%	Unit 1 – 10%	
C – 0.7% D – 17%	2 – 9%	
E – 1% F – 21%	3 – 7%	5%
G – 0.5% H – 2%	4 – 4%	
I – 7% J – 4%	5 – 2%	
K – 2%	6 – 22%	
All – 4% range 0.5 – 21%	All – 7% range 2 – 22%	

TABLE 5

Counselling

Detail for hospitals, industrial/commercial and both groups: counselling as % of the time spent directly on the patient. This excludes clerical work and work about but not with the patient. Part III of Table 3.

Hospitals	Industry/commerce	Both
A – 10% B – 10%	Unit 1 – 39%	
C – 2.6% D – 42%	2 – 24%	
E – 3.4% F – 45%	3 – 15%	
G – 1.6% H – 6%	4 – 13%	14%
I – 21% J – 11%	5 – 6%	
K – 12%	6 – 56%	
All – 11% range 1.6 – 45%	All – 20% range 6 – 56%	

Table 5 gives further details for Part III of Table 3, i.e. counselling less its clerical content, as a percentage of time in direct personal contact with the patient, not about him/her, for each individual service.

Variations in Counselling Time within the Two Groups

Hospital Group

In both Tables 4 and 5 the *lowest* amount of time spent on counselling in the hospital group was Service G, by a staff nurse, untrained in O.H., acting as such to a doctor—herself with a G.P. role for resident staff only and without proper terms of reference, or training, for O.H. work—closely followed by services C and E, in both of which the doctors did almost all the counselling. As for the highest counselling recorded in the hospital group, service F, the O.H. nurse had no O.H. training, but said she had had "years of 'giving advice' as a nursing administrator" (Assistant Matron) and apparently tended to do just that, and "medicals" (Activity 2) both activities with which she was familiar, whilst neglecting most other O.H. activities. However, service D, which had a nurse both trained and very experienced in O.H. work, cannot be accepted as the next highest, unfortunately, as the activity analysis was recorded for one day only, though all other investigations were the same as for all other services. The next highest, service I, had a very experienced O.H. nurse, holding the O.H.N. certificate, and who had set up the service about nine months before this study was done; 21% of time was spent on counselling.

Industrial/Commercial Group

(Tables 4 and 5). Here the least percentage of time spent on counselling as part of time spent with the patient was in I/C Service, Unit 5, a somewhat limited-to-treatment service, where most counselling was dealt with by another department. I/C Service, Unit 6, which was the highest, served mostly scientists in a research station where there were considerable stress factors both from the work itself and fear of imminent redundancies, although the nurse was fairly new to industry and had a combined role as Welfare Officer, which is atypical for an occupational health nurse today. Unit 1, the next highest, shows a fairly even spread of time on all O.H. activities, (see Appendix I, Table 18); 10% of all work time was spent on counselling.

Discussion

Five per cent (Table 1) of all time worked given to counselling is not high and apparently conflicts with the impression nurses have that they spend "a great deal of time" on counselling, but the impression people,

42

and particularly nurses, have of how they spend their time is often largely coloured by contact with people, and service given directly to them. The proportion of time spent directly on patients (Table 2, Part III) by both groups together, was 30·22% of all work and counselling 14·15% of this (Table 3, Part III) which is a fair portion and might well be described "as a great deal of time". This figure relates only to time spent solely on counselling and includes only part of the counselling time when something else was being done at the same time, e.g. whilst giving treatment for some physical condition, so that counselling actually occupies a larger proportion of time than stated. It is interesting to note that direct patient contact, 30·22% is not very different from that in another nursing situation. Hawthorn in her study of nurses' work (1973) found that in nine children's wards, total direct nursing care occupied 36·5% of duty time, the range being 32·8% to 44%.

The figures quoted in the above paragraphs are for the hospital and industrial/commercial services as one group, but whether of all time, or of direct patient contact, the industrial/commercial group spends twice as much of their time on counselling as the hospital group. Some hospital O.H. staff might say that they are busier than the other group and cannot spare the time, but the author does not believe this claim could be supported. In any case, less time on counselling is only true of the group as a whole—the services run by O.H. trained, experienced nurses in the hospital group—the "high" services in the rating by managers do spend a considerable amount of time on counselling. (Table 4 and Table 14 Chapter 5).

Another possible explanation of why the hospital services do less counselling is that hospital staff employees are more able to cope with their problems than those in industry or commerce. This might well be true, except for the rather curious fact that the very thing with which they might best be expected to cope, their own health, produces a greater proportion of problems to the hospital services (69%) than to the industrial/commercial services, (50%) (Tables 7 and 8). This topic needs further research into the reason for this 20% difference. It may well be that there is some truth in the frequently proffered theory that those worried about their own health seek employment in hospital as a "safe" place, or the "best place to be if anything goes wrong".

The length of time the O.H. service has been established also might affect the comparative counselling figures. With one exception, the industrial/commercial services had all been established for some years and served those who knew what to expect from the O.H. service, whilst only one hospital service had been established for more than three years. This process of awareness and acceptance takes time, and it seems to be the considered opinion among O.H. nurses (since Wright in 1916) that they are first of all judged by their professional expertise in treatment as to whether they are "any good" or not, and the word gets around! Efficiency in one direction leads to the belief in equal proficiency in other matters.

There is one other possible reason for less counselling in the hospital services. In industry and commerce an equal courtesy to all patients in the O.H. service is usual, and there is no compulsion to attend or obey. A patient in a hospital, who has come there for help with some disorder, is expected to do as he/she is told without argument, which can lead to a somewhat didactic or authoritarian approach from the staff, which is undesirable anywhere but which would certainly lead to non-co-operation from industrial/commercial employees. It is possible that this attitude to the patient may persist in the O.H. department of a hospital, where the head nurse has not worked in industry, and thus affect the number of people who present problems for counselling.

None of these suggestions to account for the difference in the proportion of counselling time between the industrial/commercial services and the hospital services can be proved without a considerable amount of further work on the subject, and this enquiry, it will be appreciated, was not among the objectives of the present study.

Section II

3.5 Problems Presented

Classification

Problems dealt with by O.H. nurses as a group, and for the hospital and industrial/commercial services separately, are detailed in Tables 6, 7 and 8. To recapitulate from Figure 3, (Chapter 2) the classifications used were:

A. *Health problems.* A1 concerning self, A2 relatives, A3 friends, A4 colleagues.

B. *Problems of personal relationships.* B1, colleagues at same level, B2 client's manager, B3 client's own staff, B4 other employees, B5 family (a) parents, (b) children, (c) spouse, (d) sibling, (e) other, B6 sex, (a) spouse, (b) male friend (c) female friend, (d) family planning (e) self, B7. other.

C. *Career or work problems.* C1 own professional development including study difficulties, C2 need for support in carrying out own job, C3 stress/frustration in own work, C4 future career/discussion—vocational guidance, C5 other.

D. *Social problems.* D1 money, D2 living accommodation, D3 travel difficulties, D4 redundancy/retirement, D5 race relations, D6 other.

44

TABLE 6

Problems presented in counselling.
All services

Total number of problems in each classification and percentage: hospital and industrial/commercial services as a group.

Code	Type	Number	% of all	% less A1–self
A	Health problems (self A1 – 927, others – 89)	975	63	13
B	Problems of personal relationships	217	14	33
C	Career or work	229	15	34
D	Social	130	8	20
	All	1,551		665

TABLE 7

Hospitals

Total number of problems in each classification: percentage of problems in each classification

Code	Type	Number	% of all	% A1
A	Health problems (A1 + self 691, others 41)	732	69	11
B	Problems of personal relationships	139	13	37
C	Career or work	135	13	36
D	Social	58	5	16
	All	1,064		373

TABLE 8

Industrial/Commercial

Total number of problems in each classification. Percentage of problems in each classification.

Code	Type	Number	% of all	%–A1
A	Health problems (A1 = self 195, others 48)	243	50	16
B	Problems of personal relationships	78	16	27
C	Career or work	94	19	32
D	Social	72	15	25
	All	487		292

Analysis

The figures in Tables 6, 7 and 8 are given both with and without A1 self/health problems, as these heavily outweigh all other problems presented. (see also Chapter 2, 2·3).

Regarding Table 6 the counselling problems dealt with by the O.H. nurses as a *single group* i.e. hospitals and industrial/commercial, totalled 1,551, of which 63% were about health, 15% career or work, 14% personal relationships and 8% social matters.

Regarding Table 7 the *hospital group* classified 1,064 problems, 69% about health, 13% career or work, 13% personal relationships and 5% social problems.

Regarding Table 8 the industrial/commercial group classified 487 problems, 50% about health, 19% career or work, 16% personal relationships and 15% social problems.

Relative Proportion of Problems as Classified into Four Groups

The highest number of problems presented in both hospital and industrial/commercial services was about *health,* very much more than any other, and most of them about the health of the client, rather than that of family, friends or colleagues. This is to be expected for O.H. nurses, just as one would expect educationalists to be presented with more problems concerning study or future career than of those concerning health.

Personal relationships and *career or work* are closely third and second respectively for both groups together, and the industrial/commercial group, but reversed for the hospital group, a negligible difference, all the variations being only 3% or less. Social problems are the lowest, for all groups.

The main difference is the higher proportion of health problems in the hospital group, (69%) compared with the industrial/commercial group, (50%). By omitting the client's own health problems, health comes last, with the other ratings virtually unchanged.

Within the group classified under "B. personal relationships" the two topics on which counselling was most often sought from the O.H. nurses were B5 concerning the family (85) and B6, to do with sexual problems (56). The breakdown for these two topics is given below in Table 9: the distribution pattern in both groups for B5, family, is very similar.

It will be noticed that the actual *numbers* for the industrial/commercial group are high (=38) considering that, in all, the six industrial/commercial services recorded only half the total problems dealt with by the eleven hospital services; this might be expected because there were fewer services in this group.

TABLE 9

Breakdown of problems of personal relationships relating to family (B5) and sexual problems (B6).

Hospitals (I), industrial/commercial (II), and both (III).

	(I) Hospitals	(II) Ind./Comm.	(III) Both
B5. Problems of personal relationships – family:			
(a) parents	15	8	23
(b) children	10	10	20
(c) spouse	16	16	32
(d) sibling	1	4	5
(e) other relatives			
classified family only	5	—	5
Total, all B5	47	38	85
B6. Problems of personal relationships – sex:			
(a) spouse	5	2	7
(b) male friend	18	2	20
(c) female friend	4	3	7
(d) family planning	16	1	17
(e) self (client's own)	2	—	2
unclassified sex only	3	—	3
Total, all B6	48	8	56

In contrast, for B6, problems concerning sexual matters, the figures for B6 (b), male friend (=18) and B6 (d) family planning (=6) are high for the hospital group compared with the industrial/commercial group (=2 and =1 respectively) even allowing for the difference in the size of the two services. Since no more than a recording of the number of problems presented was done in the present study and it was not possible to identify which problem was brought by which person, only guesses can be made concerning why in the hospital group problems about personal relations concerning a male friend B6 (b) and family planning B6 (d) should be high compared with the industrial/commercial group. It is not safe to assume that because learner nurses attend for counselling most in the hospital group, (see

Chapter 4) they are responsible for the above figures, since it is not possible to tell; nor that they are all young girls for many students are in an older age group, most pupil midwives are already SRNs and in their twenties, and "learner nurses" include many men. Nevertheless, the figures are higher, and possibly merit further enquiry.

Further confirmation of the proportions of each type of problems which were brought for counselling to O.H. nurses comes from another small study undertaken by the author in which results were very similar. This is reported in Appendix 2.

CHAPTER 4

Who Attends?

4.1 Staff Use of Counselling Services

Hospitals

Part I of Table 10 shows the proportion of the whole workforce occupied by each of the seven staff categories in the hospitals studied, a total work population of some 23,000 people, of which 3·83% presented for counselling in the twenty-day survey period. (proportion, Garton, in Monard *et al*, 1974.)

Part II shows those in each category who were counselled, expressed as a percentage of all those counselled. It might have been expected that about the same proportion of staff shown in each category in Part I would present for counselling, but Part II indicates that this is not so. It will be seen that the highest demand comes from category 3, the learner nurses and midwives, who were 10% of the workforce, but 34% of those counselled, whilst the lowest demand is from the nursing auxiliaries, category 4, and medical/dental personnel, category 1, both categories only a quarter of the number to be expected on the basis of uniform demand.

Part III shows whether less or more than expected of each group came. Trained nurses, category 2, comprise 22% of the workforce, but only 12% of those seeking counselling.

The medical/dental category proportion counselled is actually lower than all the others, because they are a higher proportion of the total workforce than is shown in Part I, as only doctors up to and including Registrars are regarded as employees and so included in these figures in Part I. Senior Registrars and upwards are contracted to the Regional Health Authority and disregarded as employees, so in fact the doctor population is higher and the proportion of them presenting for counselling (there was no discrimination in the counselling recording as to whether the doctor was an employee of the Hospital Management Committee or the Regional Health Authority,) is correspondingly lower than shown here. The correct figure is unknown, but it cannot be very different. The other categories show little difference beween observed and expected.

Because a percentage shown for any one category is higher than that of the group in the total workforce, it does not necessarily mean that all

TABLE 10

N.H.S. Staff Categories. (I) Percentage of work population, (II) Percentage counselled, (III) Less/more than expected, and (IV) Ratings, most to least.

N.H.S. Staff category	1	2	3	4	5	6	7 Unknown
I. % of each category in total work-force.*	3	22	10	13	9	10	33
II. % of all counselled.	0.7	12	34	3	11	12	26
III. less/more counselled than "expected" of each category	much less ($\frac{1}{4}$)	much less ($\frac{1}{2}$)	much more ($\times 3$)	much less ($\frac{1}{4}$)	slightly more $1\frac{1}{5}$ or 1.2	slightly more $1\frac{1}{2}$ or 1.2	slightly less $\frac{4}{5}$ths or 0.8
IV. Rating: most to least demand for counselling.	7	3	1	6	5	4	2

* Paul Garton in Monard et al. 1974.
Code: 1.Medical/dental. 2. Trained nurses, midwives. 3. Learner nurses and midwives. 4. Nursing auxiliaries. 5. Professional and technical. 6. Clerical/admin. 7. Works/domestic.

of them were counselled, only a proportion need have attended on more than one occasion to get such a result, but it could be an indication of likely demand by the group.

Part IV of Table 10, gives the rating for the categories in order, most to least, of demand for counselling according to the proportion of each group presenting for counselling.

Discussion

As has already been said, *learner nurses,* of all the N.H.S. staff categories took up most time of the hospital O.H. nurses' counselling time. Some, having come straight from school to hospital, could be immature and may well have presented with all the problems of boy friends (sometimes husbands) and parents, on top of study problems, what sort of career to follow (which specialty) and so on. The author, however, is tempted to wonder if the demand on an "official" source was as heavy when nurses in training lived together, in their sets, in a Nurses' Home, as it was at the time of this study, and thinks it unlikely. In the past, "sets", i.e. nurses who entered training at the same time, were a supportive family unit: all went on night duty or day duty at the same time and tended to be allocated rooms on the same corridor as each other in the Home—whole sets moved rooms on the same day. Then anyone coming of duty "mad at Sister", or distressed at the death of a patient, or not understanding some new nursing procedure, could almost always find someone of the same set in a nearby room from whom help could be sought and obtained, mutually sustaining, and a source of comfort, sympathy and security.

Today rooms are frequently allocated for the duration of training, so night nurses sleep on "day" corridors, the sets are split up, often in different buildings. The nurse is too proud to seek help from a junior in a neighbouring room, dares not bother a senior nurse and cannot find anyone of her own set. Even worse, nurses sometimes "live out" in bed-sitters, where they are lonelier still, and even if the hospital provides rented, self-contained flats on hospital land for two or three nurses together, they frequently do not see their flat-mates for days because of different shifts or days off, and can be extremely isolated.

In the past, it is said the Home Sister was friend and confidant to nurses who were homesick or had other problems. They were certainly kind when one was ill, but the author, having known several hospitals, never experienced this counselling function of the Home Sister, nor knows of anyone who did. The Home Sister was usually far too concerned with the details of discipline and housekeeping to have time for personal troubles, which were usually taken to a fellow student. The Sister Tutor was the "official" to whom most students turned for help in very serious matters, especially because anything necessitating

51

leave of absence had to be reported to her as training records were affected, and this still obtains today. One Senior Sister Tutor, interviewed for this study, said that she had observed a great increase in the number of students seeking counselling from her, and in the amount required, during the last few years; that is in the early 1970s. This was in a hospital where many learners were also counselled by the O.H. nurse.

Nursing auxiliaries, though they are the third largest category in the hospital workforce, attend least for counselling, and it would be possible to speculate that this is because most are married women who have the support of family and friends outside the hospital, but the same situation applies to the *works, maintenance and domestic* group, and to many of the *clerical/administrative group*, yet a greater proportion of all of these is counselled than expected according to their proportion in the workforce. The low figure for *doctors* attending for counselling is not surprising, because this record was counselling of doctors by nurses, and the traditional attitude of the one to the other must have affected the demand.

Industrial/Commercial Services Group

A corresponding analysis of the expected and observed demand for counselling from the various grades of employees was not possible for this group. (see Methods, Chapter 2)

TABLE 11

Industrial/Commercial group

Details of (I) 'works' employees attending for counselling; (II) 'staff' ditto; (III) totals.

Service Unit	1	2*	3	4	5	6	All	%
I Weekly paid i.e. 'works'	71		25	70	29	1	196	59
II Monthly paid i.e. 'staff'.	17		17	81	9	10	134	41
III Totals	88		42	151	38	11	330	—

* not recorded.

Table 11 gives the detailed numbers of each of the only two gradings possible, i.e. "works" and "staff", who attended for counselling. For reasons beyond the author's control it was not possible to note

52

proportion of works to staff in the various enterprises. It is possible only to remark that although the ratio of weekly to monthly paid employees in industry is usually regarded as approximately 10 to one, in this Table the ratio of people who attended for counselling is only about 1·5 "works" to 1·0 "staff", i.e. a sevenfold departure from the reputed "uniform" demand. The known exception to this assumed 10 to one ratio is I/C Service Unit 6, where it is known that staff outnumber work people and this is reflected in the numbers of each who attended for counselling.

Discussion

It seems that *demand cannot usefully be estimated* on the basis either of the proportion of each category in the N.H.S. nor on the "works"/"staff" category in industry/commerce, without further investigation of why people do and do not attend for counselling. If presentation for counselling is regarded as an admission that the individual needs help in coping with life's problems (and who does not?) the figures given in Table 10 and 11 *might* be helpful in estimating demand, until further research, on a much larger scale than this study, about the proportion of each group of workers which presents, and why they do so, reveals why there is this disproportionate number from various groups, enabling more accurate estimates of likely demand to be made. The same might apply to a study of different departments and comparable grades of workers in any one industrial/commercial enterprise, something which was not possible in this study because of the impossibility of comparing grades of workers in such very different enterprises, but the whole matter is very complex. It might be thought more profitable to research training for counselling, so that O.H. nurses are able to meet demands as they arise.

4.2 Men, Women, or People? (Gender)

Hospitals

Of the 1,003 people who were counselled, in 2% the sex was not recorded and of the remainder 18% were men and 80% were women, which is to be expected in a hospital population where the usual proportion is one man to four women employees. (Monard/DHSS, 1973).

TABLE 12

Gender of those Counselled. Industrial/Commercial.

(I) Proportion of men to women employees: (II) Proportion counselled:
(III) Number of men/women counselled.

	(I) Proportion employed		(II) Proportion counselled		(III) Nos. counselled	
Unit	men	women	men	women	men	women
1.	80(+ −)	20(+ −)	78.4%	21.6%	69	19
2.	not recorded		not recorded		not recorded	
3.	25	75	26.19%	73.8%	11	31
4.	50(+ −)	50(+ −)	43.06%	56.95%	65	86
5.	80	20	78.94%	21.05%	30	8
6.	80	20	81.0%	18.18%	9	2
					184	146
					=330	

Industrial/Commercial Groups

Table 12 shows the approximate proportion of men to women employed in the enterprise (column I) served by each industrial/commercial O.H. service, the proportion of each counselled (column II), together with the numbers of each counselled, (column III) for the 330 people who presented. Again demand appears to be approximately in accord with the proportions of men to women employed.

Discussion

It was said above that it "is to be expected" that demand from either sex will be equal, but in fact people generally tend to assume that it is "women who need help" and from that viewpoint it was somewhat unexpected to find that men present for counselling as much as women. Both in the industrial/commercial and the hospital groups, the proportion of either sex counselled was closely related to the proportion of each sex employed. Gender makes little difference; problems are presented by people.

CHAPTER 5

Definitions of Counselling

5.1 Classification of Concepts as held by Senior O.H. Nurses

Most of the nurses had difficulty in explaining exactly what they meant by counselling (the nurse in Hospital J refused to do so on the grounds that it was impossible) but the different items given about what was involved in counselling were listed and it was found that only one person in the hospital group and one in the industrial/commercial group expressed it in a single way, i.e. of giving advice or health education only. All the others expressed their ideas as several different items, any or all of which may be employed in "counselling" according to the need of the client. The definitions/concepts are also what has been stated to the author by a wide variety of people, including many O.H. nurses, over the past eight years, i.e. they consider counselling in the following ways:

Concept One
   (a) consists of giving advice or health education/information.
Concept Two
   (b) consists of giving advice or health education/information.
   (b) involves listening whilst the client talks or "unburdens";
   (c) client may be referred.

Concept Three
   (a) consists of giving advice or health education/information;
   (b) involves listening whilst the client talks or "unburdens";
   (c) client may be referred;
   (d) counsellor needs to present the options open to the client.

Concept Four
   (a) consists of giving advice or health education/information;
   (b) involves listening whilst the client talks or "unburdens";
   (c) client may be referred;
   (d) counsellor needs to present the options open to the client;
   (e) means encouraging *the client* to decide for himself/herself;
   (f) the giving of help and support in achieving the option, either directly or by referral to a suitable expert.

This concept would be described as an "enabling" interview, though the process could occupy more than one counselling session.

There appears to be *four levels of counselling:*—

Concept One = (a)
Concept Two = (a) + (b) (c).
Concept Three = (a) (b) (c) + (d).
Concept Four = (a) (b) (c) (d) + (e) and (f).

Two services, Hospital C and Industrial/Commercial Service Unit 4, specifically mentioned that one *never* gave advice except about health matters: both held Concept Four.

Although only those holding Concept One admit they give advice, and the others say they give advice only on health/education matters, there may be an implicit statement that participants have a tendency to advise people what to do, when they did not say they encourage the client to decide for himself/herself = (e).

Viewing these four concepts in another way, they can be associated with concepts or attitudes concerning the nurse/client relationship.

Concept One
The traditional nurse/patient role, with the nurse giving advice/information and the client passively receiving it.

Concept Two
The patient takes some part, whilst the nurse listens as they "unburden" and may either do nothing further or refer the patient to someone else.

Concept Three
The nurse shares the activity to a certain extent but leaves it to the client both to decide and/or act, once he/she has explored various ways of considering the problem and how it may be solved, i.e. the options open to the client.

Concept Four
The client takes the major role in decision making and action, whilst the nurse has an on-going supportive role, throughout. Whilst it may include the giving of straight information/explanation on health matters and such things as social service agencies, the counselling entails careful listening and encouragement to the client to "talk it out": to make decisions about priorities where there are multiple problems: at the right time and when the decision has been made by the client, aids achievement of objectives either with information or referral to more expert help, with support and encouragement throughout, as required by the client in taking any necessary action.

This last description, Concept Four, though it uses different words, is not far from the working definition "A useful definition of counselling" as formulated by the Standing Conference for the Advancement of Counselling (SCAC) for their 1969 Foundation Conference, already quoted in Chapter 1, although Gaynor Nurse's comment thereon that "conversation" implied talking, whilst listening was important, should be noted. The O.H. nurses holding Concepts Two, Three and Four, did include listening.

5.2 Analysis of Concepts Held

Table 13 shows which of the four concepts is held by the senior nurse

TABLE 13

Counselling Concepts.

Concepts held by each service, Hospitals and Industrial/Commercial.

	Concept	Hospital	Industrial/ Commercial
One.	Only giving advice or education.	G	Unit 1 ("I tell them what to do")
Two.	Advice/information/explanation, listening whilst client talks, client may be referred.	E.F.I.K.	Unit 3, 5
Three.	Advice/information/explanation, listening whilst client talks, client may be referred, options open to client presented.	A	Unit 2
Four.	Giving advice/information/expla-nation, listening whilst client talks, client may be referred,' options open to client presented, helping him to decide for himself and giving help/support either directly or by referral.	B.D.H.	Unit 6
Four a.	As 4 but specifically excluded giving advice, information as counselling.	C (Service J would not give a defini-tion).	Unit 4

Concept One was held by one hospital and one industrial/ commercial unit. Concept Two was held by four hospital and two industrial/commercial units. Concept Three was held by one hospital and one industrial/commercial unit and Concept Four was held by three hospital and two industrial/commercial units.

in each of the services studied, both hospital and industrial/commercial. *Concept One* was held by one hospital and one industrial/commercial unit. *Concept Two* was held by four hospital and two industrial/commercial units. *Concept Three* was held by one hospital and one industrial/commercial unit. *Concept Four* was held by three hospital and two industrial/commercial units.

There is no proof that where there was more than one nurse in a service those whose views were not sought, i.e. those other than the senior nurse, held the same concepts: in practice they may hold a less or more sophisticated concept than the one in charge, but it is likely that her practice would be the one followed in the service. An examination of time spent on counselling by individuals within services with more than one nurse, shows that the senior nurse, where there was one (hospital A, B, C, E: I/C service units 3, 4, 5) invariably spent more time counselling than any of the rest of the staff in that service. It may be that clients feel greater confidence in the expertise of the most senior or it may be that the senior nurse, presumably more experienced, more readily perceives an unspoken cry for help.

5.3   Discussion on Definitions/Concepts

Almost every authority has a slightly different definition of counselling and long lists of definitions can easily be compiled. In the event, the O.H. nurses participating in this study failed to provide a concensus of opinion concerning a definition of counselling, but instead described what they do when counselling.

Alexis Brooke, Consultant psychiatrist at the Tavistock Clinic, London, and elsewhere, said (1963) that there are two levels of work which tend to be described as counselling. One is the general, caring, hearing approach common to all caring, helping people. The second is deeper work, which extends right up to a third level, which belongs to psychotherapy. At the second level (at which the O.H. nurse operates in his opinion) he said training helps professional workers in fields other than psychotherapy to do counselling better. (Training in counselling skills is now more readily available to O.H. nurses.)

However, according to the view of the senior O.H. nurses, there are four levels of counselling, the most sophisticated, Concept Four, the "enabling" interview, may include giving advice/information on health matters, involves listening whilst the client talks, presents options open to the client, encourages the client to decide for himself/herself, gives help and support in achieving the chosen option, either directly or by referral to a suitable expert. The techniques for doing these things well, can be learnt.

Claire Rayner, SRN (1978) a well-known counsellor by means of the written and spoken word in the public media, said in a BBC Overseas broadcast that people come to her primarily for information, explanation and secondly, about inter-family relationships: about mothers, fathers, boys, girls. She continued:

> "I don't give advice, I try to explain both sides to each other, to get them to listen to each other, to try and get them to talk ...... I don't tell people what to do at all. I try to tidy up the mess. I say 'you have thought of ways

one and two out of it, I can think of three and four . . . . . you choose what is best to do'. They may think I've solved it, but I haven't, have I?"

Again this is a description of the O.H. nurses' Concept Four and indicates the way in which the best of them counsel.

5.4 Concepts and Characteristics of the Senior O.H. Nurse

Table 14 shows the services grouped according to the counselling concepts held. It gives, for the senior O.H. nurse, the concept held, the service code, the grade/status of the hospital O.H. service nurses (industrial/commercial grades are not comparable), the O.H. training, the O.H. experience prior to in-post appointment, length of time the post has been held, how long the service has been established, the percentage of counselling within personal patient contact, and for the hospital services only, the rating accorded to the respective O.H. services, concerning the quality of the service, held by managers of hospital departments, and the TUC Centenary Institute of Occupational Health Research Team. (For further details of the latter, see Table 16 Chapter 6.) (Monard *et al.* 1974.)

It will be noted that the most sophisticated concept of counselling, Concept Four, is held:

1. by the hospital O.H. nurses with the higher "Salmon" gradings, i.e. senior status:

2. by O.H. nurses who all had, or were studying for, the Rcn O.H.N. Certificate:

3. by those who all had O.H. nursing experience *prior* to the present appointment:

4. by those who, with one exception (industrial/commercial unit 4) had been in post since the establishment of the service, though *she* had been there for ten years of the 20 since establishment:

5. by four (out of the six services) which had been established for three years or more. I/C service Unit 6, though established only for two years on that particular site, was part of a much larger O.H. service, established for many years:

6. by those who between them had an average of 21% of counselling within personal patient contact time:

7. by those hospital services rated *high* by the N.H.S. departmental managers and the TUC Centenary Institute of Occupational Health Research Team. (See below.)

TABLE 14

Counselling concept held by/and characteristics of head nurse: age of service, rating, see table 16.

H = Hospital service   I/C = Industrial/commerical service unit.

Concept held	Service	Grade*	OHN cert.	O.H. service prior to this apptmt.	Experience in this appointment	Age of service	% counselling in personal patient contact	Managers/Team rating (opinion) H. only M = low T = high
Not given	HJ	Pr. Nsg. Officer (sole)	Yes	Yes, some	2 years	2 years	11%	M = low T = high
Concept One	HG	Staff Nurse P.T. (sole)	No	None	2 years	2 years	2%	Low
	I/C 1	Sister (sole)	Yes	None	3 years	3 years	40% 21% Av. No treatment done	
Concept Two	HE	No. 7 Dept. Head.	During appt.	None	10 years +	10 years +	3%	Medium
	HF	No. 7 Dept. Head.	No	None	2 years	2 years	45%	Medium
	HI	Sister Dept. Head (sole)	Yes	Many years	9 months	9 months	21%	High
	HK	Sister (sole)	No	None	1 year	3 years	12% Av.	Low
	I/C 3	Sister P.T.	No	None	3 years	10 years +	15% 17%	—
	I/C 5	Sister P.T.	No	None	3 years	30 years +	6%	—

Concept	Code	Title/Grade						
Concept Three	HA	Sister	Yes	Yes +	2 years	2 years	10% Av.	High
	I/C 2	Sister (sole)	Yes	Yes +	10 years +	10–15 years	24% 17%	—
Concept Four	HB	SNO 8 Dept. Head	Yes	Yes +	3 years	3 years	10%	High
	HC	SNO 8 Dept. Head	Yes	Yes ++	3 years	3 years	3% Doctor does couns.	High
	HD	Sister Grade A	Yes	Yes ++	3 years	3 years	42% Av. (one day only)	High
	HH	No. 7 pd. 6 D.H. (sole)	Yes in research	Yes +	2 years	2 years	6% 21%	High
	I/C 4	Sister I/Charge	On course	20 years +	10 years	30 years +++	13%	—
	I/C 6	Sister W.O.† (sole)	None		2 years	2 years	56%	—

* In the NHS Hospital group 'Salmon' grades are used. In the I/C group titles give no indication of grade and titles are not comparable. See also Table 16.

† W.O. = Welfare Officer

TABLE 15

Different activities within the counselling activity expressed as a % of time spent within the activity.

Activity	Hospitals	Ind./comm.	Both	Rating (both)
A. advice-medical, work, hygiene, personal	35	44	39	1
B. information and/or explanation.	12	14	13	4
C. listening.	13	21	17	2
D. supporting action including referral	16	16	16	3
E. therapeutic help	5.5	1.8	3.7	6
F. vocational guidance	2	1.4	1.8	7
G. clerical	16	2.5	9.3	5

5.5 Time Spent on Different Activities within Counselling

Regarding Table 15 an examination of the recordings on the activity analysis charts concerning time spent on different activities within counselling (activity 5) by both groups, shows that the industrial/commercial group spend more time on activity 5 (a) giving advice—medical, work, hygiene, personal, on 5 (b) information and/or explanation and on 5 (e) listening, than do the hospital group, whilst the latter (see Appendix I) spend much time on clerical work and claim to give more therapeutic help than the industrial/commercial group. It is suspected that those in the "curative" atmosphere pervading all hospitals, might consider counselling as "therapeutic" in situations which would not be so considered by those in industrial/commercial services.

With hindsight, the sub-divisions within the counselling activity on the charts, might have provided a better insight into how nurses "counsel" if the chart had been designed after analysis of their replies to the question "do you do any counselling? what do you mean by this term?" with the addition of certain items culled from the opinions of counselling experts in other fields. As it stands, however, (Table 15) the most revealing items in the recorded information is that the industrial/commercial group listens more, whilst the hospital group writes more and claim to give more therapeutic help.

5.6 General Discussion on Counselling Concepts

The difference between the modern concept of counselling which actively encourages the client to self-help and the older "telling" approach, Concept One in this study, is important. The necessary skills to achieve the former approach need acquiring by those who "counsel".

It was a surprise to be told by one excellent nurse in the I/C group, (who held Concept One) that "I get all the facts and then tell them what to do—whether they do or not is up to them". Asked whether she had had training in counselling she replied she had taken her O.H.N. certificate before counselling was taken as a separate subject in the courses, but she had read books recommended to her by a social worker friend and the friend had told her what to do. This may have been a reflection of what is said to be the difference between "counselling" by social workers and that advocated by most professional counsellors (whether psychiatrists, marriage guidance counsellors, vocational guidance personnel and many others) whose aim, in brief, is to have an enabling interview which will assist the client to deal with his own problems. To some extent, social workers have to endeavour to persuade their clients to accept what is possible within the provisions of the social services.

5.7 Health "Counselling"

What people mostly approach the O.H. nurse about concerns problems of health, the client's own health. And this often necessitates a deviation from the "true counselling" approach of no advice, because the client is seeking professional advice and explanation/information on health matters which often fall into the realms of health education which, as the Permanent Commission on Occupational Health (1969) points out "is a little different. Here the nurse is attempting to influence the behaviour of the worker in a particular direction. The effort is directed towards getting the worker to reach, not his own decision, but the decision the nurse is offering him". The sort of situation where this occurs is when the skill of the nurse (bound by the rules of confidential information) leads an epileptic to allow his close work colleagues to be told about his disability, so that they can aid his acceptance, as a normal worker, by the rest of the staff.

Where health is concerned, however, the author is aware that even in the years intervening since this survey was started, the social atmosphere has changed towards encouraging people to decide for themselves and those O.H. nurses holding Concept Four were in the vanguard of this approach. There are sound reasons for leading patients to self-help. It is probably in the best interest of the patient (and this matters more than anything else) for him to achieve a higher standard of self-help and secondly, it is economically important. If the "sick" burdens of the National Health Service are to be relieved,

63

preventive medicine is most important, and O.H. nurses have a part to play in preventive medicine by helping people to help themselves and keep themselves healthy. With improved counselling abilities, it may be that O.H. nurses could relieve medical practitioners. Doctors could refer suitable patients to the O.H. nurse, who should have the time to help them talk about the problems underlying symptoms of stress and anxiety, so that the prescription would be "counselling" instead of pills.

Knowledge that counselling is one of the services offered by an O.H. service and that staff *appear* to have time to counsel, are very important factors. Clients are reluctant to bother their own superiors they know to be very busy, or to whom they are afraid to reveal worries, and are relieved to find that there is someone who has time to listen, who is also impartial and outside the "hierarchy" of any work situation.

CHAPTER 6

The "Quality" of Counselling

6.1 Evaluation

It was possible to collect "facts" about what was done about what problems, for how much time and for whom it was done. It was not possible to enquire from the clients what the counsellor did and then compare it with what she said she did, nor to ask whether the counselling was helpful or valuable or not, because revelation that an individual had been counselled would have broken the confidentiality of the relationship. The only indications of any sort were that people *did* attend for counselling and the proportion of time spent on counselling.

Overall Quality of the Service

The overall quality of the service for each hospital in the TUCCIOH study (Monard *et al.* 1974) had been rated by the author and Dr. Paul Garton before the Departmental Managers' opinions had been assessed. No such evaluation of the industrial/commercial services was possible.

Table 16 gives the details of scores accorded to the hospital O.H. services from answers by departmental managers in a structured interview administered by members (Garton/Williams) of the TUCCIOH Team (Figure 6, Chapter 2) in column I, and in column II the subjective ratings given to these same services by team members prior to the administration of the interview with the managers. (Monard *et al.* 1974.) These two assessments coincided closely. There was disagreement between the two assessments on only one service, Hospital J, which the managers rated low but the team rated high. This was probably because the service, though established some years, had only just been extended to cover all aspects of occupational health in all departments, having previously served only nurses.

Amount of Counselling

The amount of counselling done by each O.H. service agreed to some extent with these "quality" ratings, the average counselling in the "high" assessment group (who also held Concept Four) being 21%. (Table 14 Chapter 6.) High standards of work and performance appear to equate with a high proportion of counselling in the activities of the O.H. nurse.

Further discussion about the way in which the concept held affects the way the nurse counsels, will be found in Chapter 8.

TABLE 16

Hospitals

(I) Departmental Managers' opinions of their O.H services. (II) Rating by TUCCIOH Research Team. (From Table 11.4, Monard et al. 1974)

Hospital service	Rated	(I) Total points scored	%	OHNC qualification	(II) Rating by TUCCIOH. Team
H	High	$\frac{82}{88}$	93	Yes	High
A	High	$\frac{54}{64}$	90	Yes	High
B	High	$\frac{49}{56}$	87	Yes	High
D	High	$\frac{63}{72}$	87	Yes	High
I	High	$\frac{56}{64}$	87	Yes	High
C	High	$\frac{69}{80}$	86	Yes	High
F	Medium	$\frac{56}{72}$	78	No	Medium
E	Medium	$\frac{55}{80}$	69	Yes	Medium
J	Low	$\frac{36}{56}$	64	Yes	High
K	Low	$\frac{46}{80}$	57	No	Low
G	Low	$\frac{19}{40}$	47	No	Low

Mean 74.2

Method:
Positive answers to questions 2a, 2b, 3, 5 and 6 allocated 1 point each, question 8 a chance of 3, 2 or 1 point

Equation $= \dfrac{\text{points scored} \times 100}{8 \times \text{No. of respondents}}$. (Interview numbers varied between hospitals)

For questions used for this evaluation see Fig. 6, Chap. 2.

Miscellaneous Observations Concerning Counselling made by O.H. Nurses

During interviews except for one person (who had the most limited concept of counselling, Concept One), all the nurses said that they wished "they could do it better" or "knew more about how to do it or were more skilled" and were conscious that they needed help in this function, which they neither wished to, nor could, avoid, since people turned to them for help. Only one person had had any training in counselling (Hospital B). They almost all stressed that confidentiality was essential, that it was important that there should be someone like themselves who was outside the hierarchy (whatever the client's department) and who appeared to have time.

They all said there was a need for a place, however small, which was private and soundproof, where people in distress could "let go", and some mentioned that, since appeals for help often came in the disguise of a minor ailment/injury, privacy in the treatment room was essential, as well as the provision of another place of refuge. Work-studied layouts in small treatment areas, with the nurse and patient both sitting down, not only permits privacy for the patients, and increases the number of counselling episodes, but has been proved to save nursing and employee time. (White and Cox, 1969.)

CHAPTER 7

Problems and Discussion of Effect of Counselling Concepts on Counselling Process

7.1 Typical problems

However problems are presented (often under the cover of a minor ailment), those brought to O.H. nurses are very varied and are rarely simple or straightforward. This makes classification difficult, not in deciding into which classification each problem should be placed, but in identifying the main problem (which may need to be given priority) of several. Classification areas tend to overlap. In this study there was no means of knowing which concept of counselling was used to deal with any of the problems classified under the main groups of health, personal relationships, career or work, and social problems.

The following examples illustrate the often complex nature of problems: all of them were dealt with by practising occupational health nurses, who related them to the author.

Health

A1. Self. The simplest type of problem and the most common, is one to do with the health of the client. The one quoted as an example on the classification list "I have a corn, what should I do?", calls for straight information (not counselling) on such matters as what chiropodists do, times and places of chiropody clinics, likely costs and advice about subsequent care of feet, cleanliness, pedicure, choice of socks/stockings, footwear etc., enquiry and discussion about home facilities etc., possibly finances and the need for budgetting for good footwear.

A.2 Health of Relative. An experienced O.H. nurse, looking after several plants, on one of her regular visits to a small undertaking, was immediately aware that something was not quite right. Shortly afterwards the foreman hurried to her and blurted out "Sister—is it all right if a girl of ten menstruates or could there be something wrong?" She immediately reassured him, asked a few questions about his daughter, again reassured him and asked him to come and see her later.

This interview gave him the chance to express the anxiety which had been with him for several days, how he didn't like to bother his wife (who apparently was not worried) about it, didn't like to expose his ignorance to friends, relatives or his family doctor. All this worry had upset his normally happy relationships on the shop floor, and the quality of his own performance as a foreman had fallen. He had the opportunity of relieving his feelings, of expressing his concern for his daughter, and his affection for her. The nurse got him to consider the inadvisability of "bottling it all up" and how he could have prevented his personal worry affecting his behaviour at work. The nurse mentioned how advantage could be taken in future of the information facilities offered by the O.H. service (by telephone if necessary) and by community agencies, both for himself and any member of his staff with similar problems. The incident also probably gave the nurse the idea of stressing (in induction courses or other suitable occasions), that no one can expect to know everything and there is no shame in confessing ignorance by seeking information.

A3. Health Problems of Colleagues. A senior manager of a company based in the South of England came to the nurse because he was worried about the health of a subordinate, professionally qualified and seconded to another firm, but in the North. The man's work had greatly deteriorated and he was ill with anxiety. The story was complicated. The man had been married only a short time when his wife died suddenly in the bath, of natural causes, but he had found her. After the initial shock and distress he had recovered, continued well with his work and eventually had remarried, a woman from his Southern home town. She refused to occupy his previous Northern home because of the association with the first wife and he bought a house in a nearby county. She drove to it from her home town, but on the way had a motor accident, was seriously injured and finally discharged from hospital to her mother's home in the South, to convalesce. This she did well but flatly refused to join her husband in the new home because it was in the North, and by this time she was convinced that there had been so many disasters she was sure it was unlucky for him and he must come back South. Whilst all this was going on, her mother was taken ill and hospitalized, another reason for not moving North. The manager's problem, which was causing him anxiety (and sleepless nights) was how could he help the man and still do his duty to his employers? He chose the nurse as a confidant. It would be tedious to detail the several sessions, but she let him relieve his feelings, decide which was the most urgent problem and how the others might be resolved. The manager replaced the man at the firm to which he was on loan, gave him a temporary home posting, told him he must let his new wife know that eventually he must return North, and suggested the help of the man's G.P. and the local Marriage Guidance

Council, to aid both husband and wife to come to terms, as well as telling him the O.H. nurse was available should he (the man) wish to discuss anything further. The manager also had further discussions with the O.H. nurse as further problems arose, mostly for the purpose of "blowing his top" to someone who was sympathetic and would keep confidences.

Problems of Personal Relationships
(B5. (b) (c) and B6 (a). (Family, children and spouse, and sex—spouse).

In problems of personal relationships one of the most frequent of those reported to the author, (apart from health problems) is that of the (often young) wife who in setting herself impossible objectives, becomes so exhausted that she complains frequently of malaise. Either expectations of a standard of living (food, furniture, house, clothing, automobile) are beyond the capabilities of the couple financially, or the wife's expectations of herself lead her to try to do a full time job, all the cooking, shopping, housework, laundry and still to lead a full married life with her husband. Sometimes she admits to fighting with him, coming to blows and sometimes it is he who presents, because he has "bashed" her and is shocked by his own behaviour. Such situations call for great skill in getting common sense to prevail, often entailing the involvement of outside agencies. One such man said he'd never thought about helping his wife, but having talked out what he wanted from marriage, which included nightly sex, worked out for himself how he could make this possible. Another situation is that of the middle-aged wife who is given insufficient money on which to keep the family, goes to work to provide it, is given no help with the family or the house and becomes completely exhausted in every way. Sometimes her husband presents because he is dissatisfied with the situation and can Sister recommend something, or a tonic, which will "buck her up a bit and make her like she used to be"?

Young women wanting to start a family need information about where to get help but frequently examination of the true situation and their great distress that they have not conceived, reveals they have never even stopped to think if the husband wants a family or not, what his feelings are and what he is likely to do if made a father against his wishes. Frequently the wife has had specialist medical advice without success and comes to the O.H. nurse as just another person to whom to express frustration and annoyance and in situations like this, at least the O.H. service can try to preserve the efficiency of the worker concerned by offering the opportunity to "let off steam" in confidence. Very, very occasionally a skilled counsellor's presentations of the options, and exploration of the husband's viewpoint, with referral to

70

the proper quarter in the outside agencies, may result in a satisfactory outcome for the client.

Family Planning B6.

One young woman, aged 31, came for help "what should she do, marry him or not"? He was divorced, had three young children but had had a vasectomy. She had always thought it would be lovely to have babies and was getting a bit old to delay too long, wasn't she? Enquiry and listening whilst she talked freely about this revealed she didn't really like babies at all, certainly had no interest in them until they could talk sensibly, but it might be an interesting experience to be pregnant! A few facts about what pregnancy really involved, and then a frank discussion about the young man and her feelings for him and the children, and the various options open to her, aided her decision. She married, is radiantly happy some years afterwards, is in good health, working well and coping efficiently and lovingly with the considerable problems of being a step-mother at irregular intervals, when the children come to stay.

Career or Work Problems
(C1 and C3. Professional development, future career).

A student nurse reported with a headache and wanted the O.H. nurse to say she could go off duty and to provide her with transport to the Nurse's Home, as the routine transport was not due for some hours. Apart from the statement that she had a headache, other relevant clinical signs were missing and the O.H. nurse sensed a sullen resentment about something. It transpired that the student wasn't doing too well on the ward, she was ambitious but found study difficult because she was always tired. They were short-staffed but "the others" didn't pull their weight and "went sick" whenever they felt they wanted time off for pleasure: Sister had been cross and the student didn't see why she shouldn't have time off too and anyway perhaps she'd give up nursing. The O.H. nurse had given her a mild analgesic and a cup of tea and let her talk on, but said she didn't want to send her off duty immediately because she was sure the headache would respond to treatment after a little rest. Did she really want to give up training? She could make a fight of it and show what she was made of and then decide about giving up after careful thought, not just because she was mad at "the others". After a time the nurse went back on duty, having volunteered the information that the analgesic had worked wonders. Next day she popped in to say she had felt so superior because she had "stuck it out", realized that Sister too was tired, and had thought hard about why she wanted to be a nurse, and was not going to leave.

71

Another problem concerning C1 and C4 (own professional career development, future career) was brought to a brewery O.H. nurse and presented as A2 health of a relative, and B5 (a) (c) (d), personal relationships, parent spouse, sibling. The man was employed as a manager of an hotel in the North of England, where he had always lived. He was happily settled, doing well and creating a warm friendly place which attracted many customers. He was worried about his (older) sister, who lived in the South, having moved there with their widowed mother on taking up a senior post in her chosen profession. She had had some heart trouble some years previously but made light of it, but had suddenly been hospitalized and had been told that the cardiac condition was deteriorating. His wife had gone to take care of the mother, had had an interview with the sister's consultant, who said that though the heart condition was serious, it was not acute and that the sister was really only exhausted by the demands of the mother, who let her go to work, but considered every other moment should be devoted to her. The wife returned home and the problem really was should the husband abandon his ambition to run a successful hotel and give it up, return to his former occupation and thus be able to offer a home to his mother, which was impossible in the hotel. Could Sister explain about the heart condition. Because it was a resident job, the wife was brought in and what she had been told by the consultant was listened to and discussed. It transpired that the sister had always dominated the family and done exactly what she wanted, largely ignoring the brother, his hopes and ambitions—he didn't seem to mind this much but his wife felt it was unfair that, just when he had the opportunity he had longed for, he should have to give it up, especially as the mother was very old. Having talked very freely and considered what they could do, the husband and wife decided he should keep on at the hotel and see what happened before taking any more drastic action. The wife had enlisted the help of a neighbour of the sister to relieve her on occasion, so she could go out and the O.H. nurse mentioned the possibilty of a Home Help and facilities offered by Day Centres for the elderly. The couple passed on the ideas to the sister, and the mother joined a Day Centre Club, so she was less lonely, but the problem is ongoing.

Social Problems D.

The following problem presented as "A1, self, 'fit to work'?" but this was not the real problem. A nurse, who visited a bakery once a month, was called in by the management to say if a girl was fit to do her job in the Works Canteen, the allegation by her colleagues being that she was dirty and "had a disease". They were refusing to work with her. The girl's real problem was that she and her husband and children were living in dire poverty and the classification could be said to be D1, money and D2, living accommodation. The rest of the problems were really managerial, not the girl's. The girl was clean, there was no doubt of that and fit to work in a canteen, but she looked untidy and unkempt (clothes clean but very worn) and was undernourished.

The nurse visited the canteen, which had been redecorated three months previously on the recommendation of the medical O.H. consultant, found it very dirty and it was obvious that no routine cleaning was being done at all. The manager had his dog in the office and was at odds with his wife, who was second-in-command. Both husband and wife had their own supporters in the working group. The "strike" over the girl was stopped when the nurse pronounced her fit, but in talking to the staff it came out that the girl had expressed distress to her colleagues because her home had bed-bugs which could not be got rid of. Her malnutrition and other difficulties had resulted in a slight vaginal discharge about which she had worried and had unwisely confided to an older colleague, who promptly told the manager's wife, who said "V.D." and rang the public health authorities.

The nurse felt that all she could do was to leave the administration and the necessary hygienic measure in the canteen to the manager of the firm, since it was a management matter, and set about helping the girl. She had done her best to get rid of the bed-bugs by calling in the local authority pest control officer, but unfortunately bed-bugs in that area, it was understood, were impossible to eradicate in such old property. (Apparently certain large towns in the U.K., like New York, U.S.A., have bugs which are said to be quite resistant to pesticides.) The "home" was damp and the girl, her husband and three children lived in damp, squalid conditions, without private sanitary conveniences, at high rent—yet she managed to keep both home and occupants clean. Both partners were working hard to get enough money to obtain better accommodation but it was an almost impossible task. In order to get on good terms with her workmates again, she allowed the nurse to tell them there was nothing wrong with her (the necessary tests having been done at a special clinic) and as for the girl herself, the nurse pointed out various methods by which she could deal with her work situation, among which was to make an even greater effort to improve her appearance so she *looked* better than the others. This she decided to do. It was hard for her, even though the colleagues were themselves untidy, but she did it and the friendly support of the nurse, who made herself available for discussion of problems as they arose, helped her, as did reference to a family planning clinic and a local charity which helped with clothing. Had the girl and her husband not been in such dire poverty this particular set of problems would never have arisen, but something else probably would have done in that particular firm, where the management was weak and failed to deal effectively with the canteen manager and his staff problems. The canteen remained dirty, the doctor took action and said it must be cleaned or serious trouble could result. The management took the easy way out, closed the canteen, sacked the staff and called in outside caterers. The girl obtained another canteen job without difficulty or delay, thanks to her improved appearance and confidence.

7.2 How Counselling Concepts may Affect the Counselling Process

This discussion is not based on any research findings but in the light of the four concepts held by the O.H. nurses, it is possible to postulate the effect the way in which concepts may influence the behaviour of the counsellor.

The experienced O.H. nurse is more likely to hold Concept 4, the most sophisticated and up-to-date way of counselling (see Chapter 5). It is extremely difficult to assess the quality of counselling and it is hardly possible for anyone to say the way anyone answers a request to help "is not counselling". All that one can do is to say "that way is not what professional counsellors think is the way counselling should be done". Also what O.H. nurses who have had no specialized psychiatric training can do as counsellors is, of course, limited and they would be the first to admit this. Nevertheless within these limitations and with the ability to recognize signs of mental stress requiring specialist help, O.H. nurses have a counselling role and they, like other people, can be trained how to deal with problem situations more effectively.

Taking problem C1 and C4, concerning the hotel manager with his initial query about his sister's heart complaint, as an example, if it had been brought to a holder of *Concept 1* (giving advice/health education/information), he would have received some information about heart diseases and sympathy about it, or if it had been the Sister in charge of industrial/commercial Unit 1, would have been given information, been told what to do and left to get on with it or not.

Concept 2 holders would have given him the information and listened to his worry about sister and mother and probably suggested a talk with his own or the sister's doctor.

Concept 3. The information about heart disorders would have been given and he would have been listened to and given the opportunity of verbalizing his worries about his sister and mother: he might have been referred to a doctor for further information and the nurse would have suggested the various things he could do to solve the problem, but he might have been advised to do one or another, possibly in the way which would cause least trouble to the brewery company, i.e. to stay where he was.

Concept 4. Counselling by holders of Concept 4 differs (or might have done) in that there might have been a little information and explanation about the sister's physical condition (because the detail was not specific enough) the listening would have been done but expertly enough to bring out the real worry—should he give up his cherished job? The wife would have been brought in and her feelings about the family relationship expressed and the additional information given by the sister's consultant considered. The O.H. nurse would have got the man to identify the most urgent of his problems—probably the giving up or not, of his job and what good or ill might ensue if he did either. The listing of the various parts of the whole problem situation would help him to decide which could be dealt with immediately and which could be left. The various ways of dealing with these suggested by the couple would have been added to by the O.H. nurse, for instance getting a Home Help, the sister could well afford to pay for domestic help but had not thought of it, nor of the possibility of a Day Centre once a week for company. The O.H. nurse would have made no decisions, but clarified the situation and left the couple to make decisions for themselves. She would have done her best to understand the man and his wife and have listened to what they were saying—what they were really saying. This would mean she would be attempting to counsel in accordance with the practices advocated by Gaynor Nurse and authorities such as Biestick, Paul Halmos, Carl Rogers and Ethel Venables.

CHAPTER 8

General Conclusions

The general conclusion that can be drawn from this study is that occupational health nurses spend on counselling about a *seventh of their time* given to direct personal contact with an employee. Counselling occupies 5% of all time spent on occupational health work. Nurses trained in occupational health, or those with long O.H. experience, spend a greater proportion of work time on counselling than the untrained or the inexperienced. In this study nurses in the industrial/commercial services group counselled for a proportion of their time which was twice that of those in the hospital services group.

The main difference between the two groups is that the hospital group allocated double the amount of time to clerical work than did the industrial/commercial group, but in both groups those who are better prepared spend less time on clerical work than those inexperienced in O.H. work.

Men and women present equally for counselling and do so from all grades in both hospitals and industry and commerce.

There is little difference in the proportions of the four types of problems dealt with by the hospitals group and those dealt with by the industrial/commercial group. The health of the individual was the topic on which most counselling was sought, though problems were often complex.

Concepts about counselling and the way it is done are similar in both groups, but again there is a difference between the experienced and the inexperienced in occupational health work: the former hold the more sophisticated views.

Where the opinions about counselling were sought from departmental managers in the hospital services, they wanted a confidential, impartial, "professional person" as a counsellor, who was dissociated from any management hierarchy, particularly for their private and personal problems and those which could not be taken to their superiors for fear of jeopardizing career prospects. They accepted the occupational health nurse in this role. "Want" is not necessarily "need" but occupational health nursing, like all nursing, is concerned with the patient's basic needs in life, including mental, emotional and spiritual health and comfort, as well as physical health. Counselling apparently meets a need for support in coping with the problems of life in the work situation.

The O.H. nurses all expressed the need for further instruction in how to counsel. They felt it helped their clients, and wished they had higher skills in counselling. They also emphasized the need for a place, however small, where counselling could take place in relative comfort and complete privacy of sight and sound.

All the O.H. nurses recognized that they were not the only people who could or should counsel, especially appreciating that this is one of a manager's functions, and that managers themselves often need counselling. The author met no nurse who thought that "counsellors" with no other role should be appointed, as has occurred in some hospital nursing departments (Morris, 1974) since it was felt this would encourage managers to abrogate part of their proper role. Almost everyone thought there should be someone outside the employer/employee or managerial relationship for use in certain circumstances and thought that O.H. nurses could be of particular use in this respect, a view which coincides with the Tunbridge Report (1968) on hospital O.H. services. In the hospital group, surprisingly, no one spoke of the hospital Chaplain in this role.

The ability to counsel, though many factors affect its performance, is one of the important skills of a trained occupational health nurse.

The Activity Analysis—Results, Discussion

As has already been stated in Chapter 3, for a period of 20 working days, nurses' work in 17 occupational health services was recorded, totalling some 4,730 hours, undertaken by 39 people. Eighteen full-time and 12 part-time occupational health nurses, one full-time and eight part-time clerks, participated.

For the methods used, reference should be made to Chapter 2, and for comments thereon to Chapter 3.

All activities.

The detailed findings for hospital O.H. services are shown in *Table 17** and for the industrial/commercial O.H. services in *Table 18*. *Table 1* (See Chapter 3) gives the findings for hospitals as a group, for industrial/commercial as a group, and for both groups combined, with ratings indicating the order in which most to least time is spent on each activity.

(*a*) *Hospital Services Group* (Tables 17 and 1)

The various activities are considered according to the proportion of time spent on them by the occupational health nurses.

As a group the hospital services spent *most time* on *Employee Suitability,* which includes pre and/or post employment interviews, preparation for medical examinations, arranging investigations and periodic screening but the result (28%) is weighted by three services which spent a high proportion of their time on this. (G 63%: E 50%: A 49%) but see also Table 19, clerical content. *Sick and injured* (16%) comes second, closely followed by *Departmental administration* (15%), third. The high proportion for Services B and C (30%) on this last is accounted for both by the fact much time is spent on the preparation of material for, and the writing of, advisory reports, whilst Services A, F and G did very little of this. Service I was newly established and produced its first report after this study was completed.

---

*To avoid confusion the tables in both chapters and appendices are numbered consecutively as they first appear.

The proportion of time spent on each of *various activities* (visitors, professional development, committee meetings, G.P. services and "other") nos. 10–14, was so small that these are grouped together in Table 17 (and 18) and thus (12%) came fourth. *Visitors* only occupied 0·7% of time in all the services and *General Practitioner* service, 4%, though the range was from 0·3% to 11%. This range probably reflects the difficulty of dividing the time when a patient reports (classified under sick) and is then found to be a G.P. patient of the O.H. doctor, and the nurse then spends time on what should be recorded as 13, G.P. work. In some hospital services the doctor holds a Branch Surgery and this takes the time of doctor, nurse and receptionist if there is one, the latter frequently completing the E.C. forms and other documents for the doctor. (In one service it was reported that of the doctor's daily two and a half hour session, "G.P. work usually occupied 80% of his time instead of the 46% allowed under contract, thus curtailing the time available for O.H. work on which it should have been spent." The ethical implications should perhaps be considered where money (i.e. for staff and other costs), which should be spent on all staff thus being diverted to give favourable treatment to a proportion only of the staff.)

Committees, 1% for all hospital services, occupied surprisingly little time, considering the advisory function of occupational health but this may be because the doctor sits on the committees. Both the nurses in services B and C who each spend 3% of time in committees, much more than the other services (0·02%–0·09%) have higher "Salmon" gradings, (the grading for nurses in the NHS) than the rest. *Professional development* accounted for 3·24% of time in hospital services, with a range of 0–10%. This activity included visits to other services, meetings, courses and reading journals: these are activities which are essential for occupational health nurses, because, whilst those working in other nursing fields gain information from their colleagues and from doctors and others with whom they work, the occupational health nurse and doctor are professionally isolated and have to make considerable efforts to keep up to date. This is true of all O.H. nursing practitioners but those working in hospital services reported they felt much more isolated there than they had done in industry where they possibly had been the only nurse. Only one service was provided with journals (through the hospital library) the rest obtained these at their own expense, though not all knew of the specialist journals which would help them. *"Other"* activities accounted for 4% of all time worked.

Employee protection (11%) rates next in importance as a single activity: this includes immunization at a time when a smallpox scare increased this work but Service B (6%) and those higher than the group figure (Services, A, C, D, H, I and J) spent more time on shop visits, environmental work, managerial consultation and protective clothing

79

TABLE 17

Analysis of O.H. Nursing Activities
Hospital Group

Each activity as percentage of all time worked* over twenty working days.

Activity	A	B	C	D	E	F	G	H	I	J	K	All	Range
1. Personal %*	12	9	10	5	12	12	7	8	7	9	12	10	5–12
2. Employee suitability %	49	13	3	15	50	24	63	29	9	16	18	28	3–63
3. Rehab./Restl. %	2	0.2	—	—	0.2	1	—	0.4	4	0.1	—	0.8	0–4
4. Sick/inj. %	5	30	18	27	12	14	4	25	15	21	13	16	4–29
5. Counselling %	3	4	0.7	17	1	21	0.5	2	7	4	3	4	0.5–21
6. Employee** protection %	18	6	13	22	4	9	5	12	14	19	9	11	4–22

7. Health & Hygiene Ed.%	0.8	0.4	0.7	5	—	0.5	—	4	—	—	0.7	0.6	0–4
8. Sick visits %	0.6	0.3	0.6	3.7	3	6	8	6	0.6	0.4	5	2	0.3–8
9. Department Administration %	5	30	30	7	14	6	5	10	4	11	17	15	4–30
10, 11, 12, 13 and 14. %	4	7	23	—	3	5	6	3	39***	19	22.4	12	0–39
Total hours completed	425	412	475	8	658	175	122	230	254	178	167		

No. staff

Nurses Full-time	1	2	2	1	1	—	1	1	1	1	—	} = 11/8
Nurses Part-time	1	1	—	—	4	1	—	—	—	1	1	
Clerks Full-time	—	—	—	—	—	—	—	—	—	1	—	} = 1/8
Clerks Part-time	2	1	—	1	1	1	—	—	1	1	1	

* = including meals (but excluding changing into working uniform).

** = immunization, protective clothing, shop visits, environmental surveys and managerial consultation.

*** = 36% of this 39% not classified by relief secretary.

81

matters than on immunization.

Next comes *Personal time* (10%) which is sixth. This had to be included in this study because of the rather complicated conditions of services for nurses in the National Health Service. Full-time nurses are expected to be on the premises for 43 hours 45 minutes each week, made up of $37\frac{1}{2}$ hours duty and $2\frac{1}{2}$ hours paid meal breaks (a nominal 40 hour week) plus $3\frac{3}{4}$ hours unpaid meal times. (These figures do not include changing time—unpaid.) Total meal breaks should, therefore, be $6\frac{1}{4}$ hours, 14% of all the time in the O.H. Department; the proportion is the same for part-time nurses. In all the hospital services the time taken for all personal matters was 10%, the range being from 5%–12%, that is to say, less than it should have been. They all took morning and afternoon breaks "on the job" because as one nurse said "those are their break times too and this is when they rush in to see us".

Counselling (4%) comes 7th, the range being from 0·5%–21%. This is dealt with in Chapter 3.

Rehabilitation and resettlement (0·7%) and formal health and hygiene education (0·6%) received least attention, the latter rarely being done when a service was beginning, for various reasons, including the necessity of the service "proving" itself before being accepted as a source of education for employees.

(b) *Industrial/Commercial Group.* (Tables 18 and 1)

This group spent *most time* (26%) on *sick and injured* patients, range 7%–55%. The highest, I/C Service Unit 3, (55%) was run by two part-time nurses, one of whom had had a little O.H. experience, but no training therein, and the other had had no nursing experience other than in one of the Armed Forces, which she had recently left. They worked in a factory which did high grade precision assembly work, with a low accident risk, and should be compared with I/C Service Unit 2 (26%) in a similar factory, work conditions, risks, type of worker, locality etc. were almost identical with Unit 3, except that the nurse had been there for years and was trained in O.H. nursing.

Departmental administration, (17%) rated second. Again the inexperience of the nurses in I/C Service Unit 3 (who spend 23% of their time on this) is demonstrated when compared with I/C Service Unit 2 (8%) which, as stated above is in a nearby factory, with similar hazards and work and with identical forms and other recording work for the same head office, but where the nurse was highly experienced in O.H. nursing. Within Unit 3 itself, the slightly experienced nurse took 17% of time on administration compared with the newcomer, 27%. Of course no conclusions can be drawn from only two units, but there are other indications in the A/A results from both groups that the inexperienced, untrained O.H. nurse concentrates unduly on medicals,

TABLE 18

Analysis of O.H. Nursing Activities

Industrial/commercial group

Each activity as percentage of all time worked* over twenty working days.

Activity	Units						All	Range
	1	2	3	4	5	6		
1. Personal %	7	12	3	17	10	9	12	3–17
2. Empl. suitability %	10	16	4	19	2	9	13	2–16
3. Rehab./Restl. %	6	5	1	3	—	0.31	2	0–6
4. Sick & injured %	7	26	55	18	32	24	26	7–55
5. Counselling %	10	9	7	4	2	22	7	2–22
6. Employee protection %**	12	21	6	4	41	12	13	4–41
7. Health & Hygiene Education %	10	0.1	—	0.29	—	—	1	0–10
8. Sick visits %	2	0.33	—	0.4	—	12	2	0–12
9. Dept. Admin. %	11	8	23	24	8	12	17	8–24
10, 11, 12, 13 and 14%	24	4	1	9	5	1	7	1–24
Total hours completed	127	178	210	692	248	161		

No. staff

Nurses | Full-time | 1 | 1 | – | 4 | – | 1 | = 7/4
Part-time | – | – | 2 | – | 2 | – |

No clerical help.

* = including meals (but excluding changing into working uniform).

** = immunization, protective clothing, shop visits, environmental surveys and managerial consultation.

clerical work, etc. with very little attention to preventive measure other than immunization, i.e. they busy themselves with things they know how to do!

Third for the industrial/commercial group is *Employee suitability,* (13%) coupled with *Employee protection,* also 13%, though the uncorrected figures show an insignificant advantage to protection: 13·1% compared with 12·6%.

Fifth is *Personal time* (12%, range 3–17%). I/C Service Unit 3, with the highest amount had to take full meal breaks, since the whole works closed for lunch. This group too took morning and afternoon breaks "on the job", usually in case conferences if there were no patients. Unlike the hospital group it was not possible to calculate an exact proportion of time allowed for meals for this group, as customs and hours of work varied from enterprise to enterprise and it is not possible to comment on whether they took full meal breaks or not. The low figure for I/C Service Unit 3 is because the hours of duty for both part-time nurses only included short morning and afternoon breaks, no full meal time.

Counselling comes sixth (7%, range 2–22%) and is fully discussed in Chapter 3, Tables 3, 4 and 5. Counselling shares its position with the *Group of activities* nos. 10–14 (7%, range 1–24%). Visitors take 1% and "other" 2% .

Rehabilitation and resettlement, 2%, together with *Sick Visits* (2%) comes eighth and again formal *Health and hygiene education* (1%) received least attention of all.

(c) Comparison of the Two Groups

As already mentioned in Chapter 3, many factors determine the proportion of time given by an O.H. service to any one activity. None of these results should be taken to indicate an "ideal" allocation, but every O.H. service should allocate some time to activities 2–12, with the possible exception of activity 8, sick visiting. However, the "better" services in both hospital and industrial/commercial groups spread their time fairly well over all the activities, and the results given probably indicate fairly accurately how many O.H. nurses in the U.K. spend their time.

Table 1, (Chapter 3) gives details of the comparison between the two groups and of both together as a single group. The combined group ratings (most to least) for each activity shows a slight rearrangement of the ratings of the various activities. Employee suitability comes first, sick and injured second but there is very little difference between them. There is, however, *one main difference* between the two groups and this relates to the amount of clerical work performed, and secondly, to the percentage of time spent on counselling.

(i) The greatest difference in practice between the two groups is in the amount of time spent on *Employment suitability*. The hospital group's 28% is more than twice as much as the industrial/commercial group's 13% but this difference is because the hospital services spend so much time on clerical work for this activity. Indeed, this is true in all their activities.

The Amount of Clerical Work

Table 19 gives *details concerning Activity 2, Employee suitability,* which is the activity on which the hospitals (28%) spent most time. The industrial/commercial services spent only 13% of time on this activity, a higher proportion being spent on the care of the sick and injured. However, the breakdown of Activity 2 into its component parts in this table reveals that the hospitals spent more time writing about it than

TABLE 19

Activity No. 2, Employee Suitability:

Percentage of time spent on each part within the activity itself.

(NB. Table 1 shows biggest difference in % of time spent between hospitals and industrial/commercial group is in activity 2, employee suitability: hospitals 28%, I/C 13% of all time worked.)

Act. 2.	Classification of employee suitability	Hospitals	I/C
2a + b	Post/pre employment interview + preparation for medical examination	35%	53%
2c	Arranging investigation	1.5%	12%
2d	Periodic screening	7%	19%
2e	Clerical work	54%	15%
2	Not classified	3%	2%
Clerical content of Act. 2 as % of all time worked		16%	2%

the industrial/commercial group—54% against 15%—and indeed more on writing about it than actually doing the activity proper. (46%.) If clerical work is deducted, the proportion of time spent on Activity 2 by the two groups is comparable. (Hospitals 28%—16% = 12%, I/C 13%—2% = 11%)

Table 20, Part I, gives details of the proportion of time devoted by the hospital services (individually and as a group) to clerical work for each activity as a percentage of all activities. Part II gives the ratings, most to least, together with clerical work for each activity as a percentage of all their clerical work. The hospitals spent most clerical time (15%) on employee suitability, with departmental administration and sick and injured (5%) second.

Table 21 gives the same information as Table 19 but for the industrial/commercial services. This group spent most clerical time (7%) on sick and injured. Again departmental administration (5%) came second.

Table 22 gives comparative figures of clerical work for (I) the hospital group, (II) the industrial/commercial group and (III) both together as a percentage of all time worked for each activity, with ratings most to least.

Table 23 gives clerical time for each activity as a percentage of all time on clerical work, for the hospital group, the industrial/commercial group, and both together, with ratings for each, most to least.

The reasons for this pre-occupation with clerical work in the hospital services are not immediately apparent nor certain, particularly as the hospitals spend *less* time compiling and writing reports for

85

TABLE 20

Hospitals: clerical content of activities

Detail of time on clerical work expressed (I) as % of all time worked, for each activity for each hospital service and as a group; and (II) the group clerical work for each activity as % of all their clerical work, with rating, most to least.

Activity	I Hospitals %												II % Rating	
	A	B	C	D	E	F	G	H	I	J	K	All	%	Rating
1. Personal*	NIL													
2. Empl. suitability	32	5	0.8	6	28	13	32	18	1	4	8	15	46	1
3. Rehab. & Restl.	NIL													
4. Sick/inj.	1	3	4	12	7	4	0.2	12	3	6	8	5	15	3
5. Counselling	0.3	0.3	0.1	—	0.1	6	—	0.3	1	0.2	—	0.6	2	8
6. Employee protection**	NIL													
7. Hlth. Hyg. Education	5	0.5	3	—	0.5	1	2	0.5	0.3	8	0.4	2	6	5
8. Sick visits	—	0.12	—	—	3	3	0.3	1	0.19	0.04	3	1	3	6
9. Dept. admin.	0.2	16	10	7	5	2	0.2	2	1	5	2	5	16	2
10. Visitors	NIL													
11. Prof. dev.	0.07	0.06	3	—	0.3	—	—	0.3	1	0.2	—	1	2	7
12. Committees	NIL													
13. G.P. serv.	NIL													
14.	—	—	—	—	—	—	—	—	***36	—	11	4	11	4
Total clerical	39	25	21	24	43	27	35	34	43	24	31	33		

*including meals.   **immunization,   protective   clothing,   shop   visits,   environmental   surveys   and   managerial   consultation.
***Secretary away, done by N.O.

TABLE 21

Industry & commerce: Clerical content of activities

Detail of time on clerical work expressed as (I) % of all time worked for each activity for each service, and as a group: and (II) the group clerical work as a % of all their clerical work, for each activity, with rating, most to least.

Activity	(I) Industry & commerce						All	(II) All: % of all clerical time	Rating
	1	2	3	4	5	6			
1. Personal			NIL						
2. Employee suitability	2	1	0.5	2	0.3	5	2	12	3
3. Rehab./Restl.		NIL							
4. Sick & injured	2	11	18	6	1	6	7	46	1
5. Counselling	1	—	—	0.1	0.3	—	0.2	1.2	7
6. Empl. protection**	1	1	2	0.3	—	1	1	3	4
7. Hlth, Hyg. Ed.			NIL						
8. Sick visits	1	0.3	—	—	—	1	0.24	2	6
9. Dept. Admin.	5	2	7	8	0.3	0.4	5	33	2
10. Visitors			NIL						
11. Prof. development	1	—	—	1	—	—	0.32	2	5
12, 13 & 14			NIL						
Total clerical work	13	14	27	17	2	14	15		

** immunization, protective clothing, shop visits, environmental surveys, managerial consultation.

87

TABLE 22

Clerical content of activities

Hospitals, industry/commerce, and both; clerical work as % of all time worked, for each activity, with ratings, most to least.

Activity	(I) Hospitals %	Rating	(II) Ind./commerce %	Rating	(III) Both %	Rating
1. Personal	Nil	—	Nil	—	Nil	—
2. Employee suitability %	15	1	2	3	11	1
3. Rehab./Restl.	Nil	—	Nil	—	Nil	—
4. Sick & inj. %	5	2	7	1	6	2
5. Counselling %	1	6	0.2	7	0.4	8
6. Employee protection**	2	5	1	4	1	5
7. Hlth, Hyg. Ed.	Nil	—	Nil	—	Nil	—
8. Sick visits	1	6	0.2	6	1	5
9. Dept. admin.	5	2	5	2	5	3
10. Visitors	Nil	—	Nil	—	Nil	—
11. Professional development.	1	6	0.3	5	1	5
12. Committees	Nil	—	Nil	—	Nil	—
13. G.P.	Nil	—	Nil	—	Nil	—
14. Other	4	4	Nil	—	2	4
Totals All clerical work	33%		15%		27%	

management about their work than the industrial/commercial group. One reason could be that more clerks were employed in the hospital group—only three services were without clerical help, whilst the industrial/commercial group services had none—except that the hospital spending the highest proportion of time on clerical work, (E 43% Table 19 p 85) had no clerks at all. It is not known what proportion of (now existing) NHS O.H. services have clerical assistance, nor how this proportion compares with services in industry and commerce. It may have been pure chance that none of the industrial/commercial group had clerical help, or it may not. Many firms realise that nurses can be relieved of some essential record-keeping chores by the use of clerical help, leaving the nurse to do only those of a highly confidential nature. This whole matter may possibly merit further investigation.

Two other possible reasons for so much clerical work are, *firstly* inexperienced persons, insecure in a situation where they lack

TABLE 23

All hospitals, all industrial/commercial and both; clerical time for each activity as % of all time on clerical work, and ratings.

Activity	I Hospitals %	Rating	II Ind./comm %	Rating	III Both %	Rating
1. Personal	—	9	—	8	9	9
2. Employee suitability	46	1	12	3	43	1
3. Rehabilitation & resettlement	—	9	—	8	—	9
4. Sick & injured	15	3	46	1	23	2
5. Counselling	1.8	7	1.2	7	1.8	8
6. Employee protection	5.6	5	3.4	4	5.6	4
7. Health & Hygiene education	—	9	—	8	—	9
8. Sick visits	2.9	8	1.6	6	2.9	7
9. Departmental admin.	16	2	33	2	21	3
10. Visitors	—	9	—	8	—	9
11. Professional development	1.9	6	2.2	5	2.1	6
12. Committees	—	9	—	8	—	9
13. G.P. service	1.5	4	—	8	1.5	8
14. Other	3.5	9	—	8	3.5	5

knowledge of the work which should be done, tend to fill time with tasks with which they are familiar—in the nursing field, "medicals", treatment and keeping records, leaving them too busy for unfamiliar work.

Secondly, even the experienced O.H. nurse has been conditioned to the traditional or habitual practice of hospital nurses to record data by old-fashioned methods, handwritten lists and reports copied into bound books, though this is now changing in some places. Apparently little account has been taken by the authorities of the cost and inefficiency of such practices.

Nurses who work outside hospitals are possibly more aware of modern methods and concepts and incorporate these ideas in their own work. The "better" hospital services, (Tables 14 and 16) led by nurses trained in O.H. and taught to ask "why is this being recorded?" and "is this the best way of doing it?" and with experience outside hospitals, spend less time clerking than those who have never or only recently left hospital work. Results from one "better" hospital, Service A, with a well qualified and experienced head nurse, apparently refute this statement, (Table 20) but there are reasons for this. She was burdened by an "inherited" colleague who had been Home Sister for many years, spent *all* her time on "medicals" and clerical work and flatly refused to change. In addition clerical work by nursing staff of this hospital was antiquated and changes were resisted. With the exception of the Nursing Department, all other managers sent copies of sickness certificates to the O.H. Department. For nurses, the senior O.H. nurse had each week to hand-copy from a list in a book written by and kept in the office of a very senior nursing administrator—which took a total of $1\frac{3}{4}$ hours—and on return to the O.H. department transcribed the details to individual patient records. One can only comment further that a photocopy of each certificate, filed in the patient's envelope (with perhaps a date stamp on the patient's attendance card to indicate its presence) is all that an O.H. Department needs for most patients. When the O.H. medical officer or nurse require details of a particular person, it is a few seconds' work to assemble the information from the copy certificates. It is the function of Finance or Personnel Departments to provide sickness and other absence rates for comment by the O.H. Department, not that of the O.H. Department.

It also appears that the longer a nurse has been away from hospital conditions, the less clerical work may be done. Again reference to industrial/commercial Units 2 and 3 may be made. These were separate but similar factories in the same Company, keeping identical records, yet Unit 3 spent 27% of all time on clerical work, compared with 14% by Unit 2, which had an O.H. qualified, very experienced O.H. nurse and while Unit 3 was staffed by two part-time nurses, neither qualified nor experienced in O.H.

(*ii*) *The next largest difference* in practice between the two groups is in counselling (Activity 5) where the industrial/commercial group do almost twice as much as the hospitals, though the difference is insignificant as a percentage of all time worked, but not of direct patient time. (Chapter 3, see Table 1, Table 2, and Table 3.)

The third largest difference in practice is in the treatment of sick and injured (Activity 4). In this the hospitals also spent less time than the industrial/commercial group, which might be expected as there *may* be more self-diagnosis and opportunities for self-treatment in hospital and fewer traumatic hazards than in industry. However, those spending the highest proportion of time on the sick and injured in the hospital group, were hospitals B (30%), D (27%), H (25%) and J (21%) and these are nearer to the results of the industrial/commercial group. They were all run by experienced, trained O.H. nurses. The suspicion is that their expertise in other O.H. matters, might encourage employees to report injuries because of the realization that these O.H.

departments are interested in identifying and eradicating causes of injury and sickness and so increase the time spent on it. It is as bad for an O.H. nurse to spend time tying up cut fingers without finding out why they are cut and remedying it through management, as it is to do "medicals" but not know the parameters, physical, mental and emotional, of the job the person is going to do, or the conditions under which it will be done.

General Conclusion

The conclusion concerning how O.H. nurses spend their time is that the better services in both the hospital and industrial/commercial groups spread their time fairly well over all the activities, the exact proportion varying according to their situation, but that rehabilitation and resettlement, health and hygiene education tend to be neglected in both groups. There is a tendency for the untrained, inexperienced O.H. nurse to do the familiar tasks at the expense of new skills essential to O.H. nursing work.

APPENDIX 2

A Further Study of Counselling Problems

Data collected at Rcn Institute of Advanced Nursing Education Study Course, Keele University, April 1976.

In 1976 the author acted as leader of a syndicate at a Rcn Institute of Advanced Nursing Education O.H. Nursing Study Course, held at the University of Keele, which discussed "Counselling—the ethical approach to practical problems". Members of all syndicates had to do some work in advance of the course. For the counselling syndicate, in order to assist them to clarify their ideas, part of this work was to classify counselling problems for five consecutive days prior to the course, using the same classifications as in the author's present study. (For details of preparatory work see below.)

Returns were·obtained from eight different syndicate members, representing enterprises doing: precision assembly work; smelting; scientific research; producing fertilizers; pharmaceuticals; food; and two nationalized industries. The number of problems was 222, presented by 143 people, 95 men and 48 women, 88 weekly paid and 55 paid monthly. Table 24 shows the results from the Keele syndicates,

TABLE 24

'Keele' group compared with the % of problems presented, hospitals (Table 7), industrial/commercial group (Table 8): % in each classification, for each group and ratings (most to least).

Group	A. Health		B. Personal relation- ships		C. Work/ career		D. Social	
	%	Rating	%	Rating	%	Rating	%	Rating
Keele	61	(1)	17	(2)	13	(3)	9	(4)
Hospitals	69	(1)	13	(2)	13	(3)	5	(4)
Industrial/ commercial	50	(1)	16	(3)	19	(2)	15	(4)

92

totalled under each classification, compared with the hospitals, (Table 7) and the industrial/commercial services, (Table 8), with which there is close agreement.

The Keele group counselled most on health problems, but if those concerning A1, health of the client, were omitted, health rated last, and the others were in the same order as before with personal relationships, work/career and social problems, in that order.

Preparatory work for O.H. nurses attending Royal College of Nursing Occupational Health Nursing Study Course, University of Keele, April 1976. Syndicate No. 5. "Counselling—the ethical approach to practical problems".

In a recent survey all the occupational health nurses were expected to "counsel" and all wanted to improve their skill—to learn how to do it better (Monard, Garton, Williams, 1974).

It is quite impossible to achieve this in one session but whatever the state of our expertise, we can start the improvement process by discussion and exploration of the topic. Time will be saved if some preparatory work is done by all syndicate members in advance so please turn this page over and on it :–

(1) Write down what you now mean when you use the word "counselling" as one of your own activities;
"counselling" is . . . . i.e. *the definition.*

NOW, without reading any further :—

(2) List down what you now think you do when you counsel someone, i.e. *the process.*

NOW READ ON!

93

(3) As soon as possible, for a period of five working days (preferably consecutive days) make a note of all the people you counsel during your normal working day, under the heading given below. (You may be treating them physically at the same time you are counselling, or it may be in the canteen!)

Male/female (No names but something to remind *you* of the case.)	*Approx. age*	*Work status.* (operative or staff)	*Problem classification*

A. HEALTH PROBLEMS

1. concerning self, including straight information answering a question like "I have a corn, what should I do?"
2. of relatives.
3. of friends
4. of colleagues.

B. PROBLEMS OF PERSONAL RELATIONSHIPS

1. colleagues at same level.
2. client's "manager".
3. client's own staff.
4. other employees.
5. Family (a) parents
        (b) children
        (c) spouse
        (d) sibling
        (e) other relatives
6. Sex (a) spouse
        (b) male friend
        (c) female friend
        (d) family planning
        (e) self
7. other

C. CAREER OR WORK PROBLEMS

1. own professional development including study difficulties.
2. need for support in carrying out own job.
3. stress/frustration in own work.
4. future career/discussion—vocational guidance.
5. other.

D. SOCIAL PROBLEMS

1. money.
2. living accommodation.
3. travel difficulties.
4. redundancy/retirement.
5. race relations.
6. others.

(Put a line between to separate the days. For your own interest you might like to note your total case load for each day and we can work out what % of all were counselled.)

(4)   Bring this record with you to Keele and hand it in before Tuesday lunch time.

(5)   When you are making all these notes, try to find time then or later to remind yourself what you did in each piece of counselling, so that you are *actively thinking* about your own role. To give examples would defeat the object as it is *your* concepts, *your* thoughts, motives, which you are examining.

(6)   If any problem raised special difficulties for you, note the case details so we can share it at Keele.

(7)   Finally, just before you leave for Keele, again write down what you now think is the definition of counselling—which may be the same as the one you first wrote down or may be different because you have been analysing your own actions and thoughts. And also list the process again, if it is different from the first one.

This means we shall have some facts on which to work and shall have given considerable thought to it in advance, and can explore together the ethics of how we deal with the problems, (which are brought to us) and where we can get further help.

Author's note. These nurses also experienced all the difficulties in defining "counselling" referred to in Chapter 5, and those who did attempt it, also made a list of what they did, rather than writing a definition.

References

ALTSCHUL, A., EVEREST, R., GUTTRIDGE, and SCHOENFELD, M. (1964) How nurse tutors use their time. *Nursing Times* June 5, 1964, pp. 744–745.

AMERICAN ASSOCIATION OF INDUSTRIAL NURSES (1949) *The industrial nurse. Her duties and responsibilities.* Distributed for the A.A.I.N. by the Federal Security Agency, Public Health Service, Washington D.C.

AMERICAN MEDICAL ASSOCIATION (1943) Council on industrial health. Standing Orders for nurses in industry. *Jnl. Am. Med. Assoc.* Aug. 28, 1943, vol. 122 pp. 1247–1249.

BEDFORD GENERAL HOSPITAL, *Occupational Health Service Annual Reports,* (1967–1974) Bedford Group Hospital Management Committee— (changed to Bedfordshire Area Health Authority, Northern District 1st April 1974)

BRIGGS REPORT: (1972) *Report of the Committee on Nursing:* Cmnd. 5115, HMSO, London.

BROOKE, A. (1973) *"Counselling" in occupational health nursing:* Rcn Occupational Health Annual Conference.

BROWN, M. L. (1969) *Occupational health nursing in the United States: training and education.* Symposium held during the International Occupational Safety and Health Congress, Geneva, 1969; I.L.O. Occupational Safety and Health Series No. 23., p. 61, Geneva, 1970.

BUNDLE, N. (1973) Senior Occupational Health Nurse, Division of Occupational Health and Pollution Control, Health Commission of New South Wales, Australia (*Personal communication,* 21 August 1973)

CHARLEY, I. (1954) *The birth of industrial nursing.* Baillière Tindall, London. (reprinted 1978)

COPPLESTONE, J. (1967) *Preventive aspects of occupational health nursing.* Ed. Arnold, London.

DOWSON-WEISSKOPF, A. B. (1944) *Industrial nursing, it aims and practice.* Ed. Arnold, London.

FRENCH, M. (1968) *Nurses' contribution to the health of the worker with regard to counselling and liaison with Departments and outside Agencies.* Paper read to meeting of the Nursing Sub-Committee of the Permanent Commission and International Association on Occupational Health, London, October 1968. (*Personal communication.*)

GARTON, P. (1973) *Personal communication.* TUC Centenary Institute of Occupational Health, London School of Hygiene and Tropical Medicine.

HARDY, M. (1967) *Occupational health nursing in Ontario.* Report on results from questionnaire, Ontario Dept. of Health, Environmental Health Branch, Toronto.

HAWKINS, G. M. (1973) Counselling, the nurse's role. *Occ. Hlth,* Vol. 23: No 6: pp. 223–226.

HAWTHORN, P. J. (1973) *Nurse, I want by mummy!* Study of nursing care project, Series 1, No. 3. Royal College of Nursing, London, p. 54.
HENRIKSEN, H., (1959) *Curriculum study of the occupational health nursing—an adventure in co-operation.* Sponsoring Agencies, The American Journal of Nursing Company and The Minnesota League for Nursing, Minnesota.
HODGSON, V. H. (1933) *Public health nursing in industry.* Macmillan Company, New York.
HOXTER, H. Z. (1974) *Counselling developments—the national scene.* Rcn Conference, Staff Counselling for Nurses, June 1974.
INDUSTRIAL NURSING SECTION EXECUTIVE COMMITTEE (1943) *National Organization for Public Health Nursing.* Functions of nurses in industry. *Public Health Nursing,* November 1943.
INTERNATIONAL COUNCIL OF NURSES, 1952/6. See Pemberton
INTERNATIONAL LABOUR ORGANIZATION/WORLD HEALTH ORGANIZATION, ILO/WHO, (1957) Joint *Seminar on the nurse in industry,* London, WHO, Regional Office for Europe, Copenhagen.
INTERNATIONAL LABOUR ORGANIZATION. (1969) *Occupational Safety and Health* Series No. 23, Geneva, 1970.
JAMES, M., J. O'BRIEN, M. E., ELDER, D. L. and MARRIOTT, F. P. (1970) *Survey of Occupational Health Practices by nurses in Victoria, Australia.* XVI Congress, Permanent Commission and International Association on Occupational Health, Proceedings, p. 770, published by Organizing Committee, Tokyo, Japan, 1971.
JOINT ILO/WHO—see ILO/WHO.
JOLLEY, J. L. (1968) *Data Study.* Weidenfeld & Nicholson, London.
KEARNS, J. L. (*et al,* 24 in number) (1973) What is counselling? *Occ. Hlth:* Vol. 25: No. 5. pp. 176–181.
KELLER, M. L. and MAY, W. (1970) *Occupational health content in baccalaureate nursing education.* U.S. Dept. of Health, Education & Welfare, Cincinnati.
LEE, J. (1978) *The new nurse in industry.* National Institute for Occupational Safety and Health, (NIOSH) U.S. Dept. of Health, Education and Welfare, Cincinnati.
McGRATH, B. J. (1946) *Nursing in commerce and industry.* The Commonwealth Fund, New York.
METROPOLITAN LIFE INSURANCE COMPANY (1962) *Correlated activities in an employee health program.* MLIC, New York.
MONARD, P. (1973) *Private communication:* figures obtained by him from Dept. of Health and Social Security. TUC Centenary Institute of Occupational Health, London School of Hygiene and Tropical Medicine.
MONARD, P., GARTON, P., WILLIAMS, M. and TAYLOR, P. (1974) *The care of the health of hospital staff.* Report on a survey of hospital occupational health services in England and Wales (to DHSS) TUC Centenary Institute of Occupational Health, London School of Hygiene and Tropical Medicine.
MORRIS, P. (1974) *Counselling Nursing Staff* (St. Thomas Hospital, London) Rcn Conference on Staff Counselling for Nurses, June 1974.
NATIONAL BOOK LEAGUE (1973) *Counselling and guidance:* an annotated list. National Book League, London.

NATIONAL INSTITUTE OF OCCUPATIONAL SAFETY & HEALTH (NIOSH) (1975) *Hospital occupational health services study,* Part I, Appendix A, p. 50 and Part V, p. 3. *O.H. services for hospital employees.* U.S. Department of Health, Education and Welfare, Cincinnati.

NATIONAL ORGANIZATION FOR PUBLIC HEALTH NURSING, Industrial Nurses Section Executive Committee (1943) Functions of nurses in industry. *Public Health Nursing,* November 1943.

NURSE, G. (1975) *Counselling and the nurse.* Topics in Community Health series, H.M. + M. Publishers, Aylesbury, and *personal interview,* 26 November 1975.

NURSING SUB-COMMITTEE PERMANENT COMMISSION AND INTERNATIONAL ASSOCIATION ON OCCUPATIONAL HEALTH, 1969 and 1973, see Permanent Commission. *Occ. Hlth.,* Vol. 25; No. 2., p. 47.

OKUI, YUKIKO. (1975) *Health counselling by occupational health nurses.* XVIII Congress Permanent Commission and International Association on Occupational Health, Brighton, 1975. Abstracts, (no Proceedings) pp. 76–77, and *personal communication, 1975.*

PEMBERTON, D. (1952) *Acceptable standards of industrial nursing service.* Report to the Nursing Service Committee, International Council of Nurses, 1952. Up-dated by M.M. Williams and published under title Occupational Health Nursing, *International Nursing Review,* Vol. 3; No 1, pp. 49–64. 1956.

PEMBERTON, D. (1965) *Essentials of Occupational Health Nursing.* Arlington Books, London.

PERMANENT COMMISSION AND INTERNATIONAL ASSOCIATION ON OCCUPATIONAL HEALTH, (1969) *The nurse's contribution to the health of the worker.* Report of the Nursing Sub-Committee, 1966–9, No. 1, October 1969; No. 2, *Ditto, Education of the nurse.* October 1973. London, Treasurer, Permanent Commission Nursing Committee, c/o Rcn, London.

PUBLIC HEALTH NURSING SECTION, AMERICAN PUBLIC HEALTH ASSOCIATION (1942) To study the duties of nurses in industry: Committee organized 1940. Year Book, 1942—supplement to *American Journal of Public Health,* Vol. 32: No. 3. March 1942.

RAYNER, C. (1978) *Counselling.* B.B.C. Overseas Service Broadcast, 9 September 1978, confirmed by personal communication.

ROYAL COLLEGE OF NURSING, (1964 to date) Booklets and information leaflets issued by the Occupational Health Department, to members and others, including the Rcn Occupational Health Committee publications *Occupational Health Nursing Structure,* May 1968, revised 1971 and *Occupational Health Nursing, 1968.*
(1964) *A hospital occupational health service.* Memorandum presented to H.M. Government, 1964, Nursing Times, Nov. 27, 1964.
(1967) *The State Enrolled Nurse in charge of an occupational health unit.* (Proposed training programme) O.H. Department, December, 1967.
(1968) *The implementation of a hospital occupational health service, July 1968.*
(1968) *Education for O.H. nursing.* Results of a survey by the O.H. Department, March 1968.
(1975) *Guide to an Occupational Health Nursing Service.* A handbook for employers and nurses, May 1975.

(1978) *Counselling in nursing*. Report of a Working Party. (under aegis of Rcn Institute of Advanced Nursing Education) 1978.

ROYAL SOCIETY OF MEDICINE, (1972) *Occupational health services in hospitals*. Proceedings, Vol. 65. May 1972.

SCHILLING, R. S. F. *Occupational Health Practice*. (1973—revised 1980) (Chap. 3, pp. 46–7.) Butterworths.

SPRINGER ORGANIZATION, FRANKFURT, (1973) *personal communication* from the O.H. nurse at "de Spiegel", October 1973.

STOVES, V. (1970) *Occupational health nursing*. Symposium held during I.L.O. International Occupational Safety and Health Congress, Geneva, 1969, entitled "The occupational health nurse", I.L.O. Occupational Safety and Health Series No. 23, p. 5. I.L.O. Geneva.

TUC CENTENARY INSTITUTE OF OCCUPATIONAL HEALTH, LONDON SCHOOL OF HYGIENE AND TROPICAL MEDICINE, (1974) *Report on "The care of the health of hospital staff"* (Monard *et al, 1974*).

TUNBRIDGE REPORT (1968) *The care of the health of hospital staff*. Report of the Joint Committee, to Ministry of Health, Scottish Home & Health Department, Central and Scottish Health Services Councils, HMSO, London.

TYRER, F. H. (1961) *Occupational health nursing*. Baillière, Tindall, London.

UNITED STATES PUBLIC HEALTH SERVICE BULLETIN (1944) No. 283, *Nursing practice in industry*. Federal Security Agency, U.S. Public Health Service, Washington, D.C.

WAGNER, S. (1957) *Industrial nursing and its future*. Proceedings, XII Permanent Commission and International Association, International Congress on Occupational Health, Helsinki, p. 525, July 1957. (1941–62)

WEST, M. M. (1941 and 1949) *Handbook for industrial nurses*. Ed. Arnold, London. *A handbook for occupational health nurses*. 1962 Ed. Arnold, London.

WHITE, C. AND COX, M. R., (1965) Work study in the development of a dressing unit. *Occ. Hlth*. Vol. XVII, No. 6, June 1965, p. 69 et seq.

WORLD HEALTH ORGANIZATION, (1950) *Report of an Expert Committee on Nursing*, WHO, Geneva, 1950.

WRIGHT, F. (1916) *The visiting nurse in industrial welfare work*. National Safety Council, Detroit, 1916 *and (1920). Industrial nursing—for industrial, public health and pupil nurses and for employers of labour*. Macmillan, New York, 1920.

Bibliography

ADAMS, J. F. (1962) *Problems in counselling.* Macmillan, New York.
AUTTON, N. (1967) *The pastoral care of the bereaved.* Society for the Propagation of the Gospel, London.
ARGYLE, M. (1973) *The psychology of interpersonal behaviour.* Penguin, London.
BARNARD, J. M. (1975) The links with community nursing. *Nursing Mirror* September 11th.
BESSELL, R. (1971) *Interviewing and counselling.* Batsford, London.
BEVERIDGE, W. E. (1968) *Problem solving interviews.* Allen & Unwin, London.
BIESTEK, F. P. (1965) *The casework relationship.* Allen & Unwin, London.
BIRCH, J. (1975) *To nurse or not to nurse.* Royal College of Nursing, London.
BLACKHAM, H. J. (1974) *Ethical standards in counselling.* Standing Conference for the Advancement of Counselling, London. (Bedford Square Press/National Council of Social Service).
BRIDGER, H AND MILLER, E. J. (1963) The doctor and sister in industry. *Occ. Hlth.* Vol. XV Nos. 5 & 6 (Macmillan Journals, London—Now Baillière, Tindall).
DICKENS, M. (1970) *The listeners.* Heinemann, London.
ELDRED, A. C. (1967) All nurses should be counselors *Journal of Occupational Health Nursing.* (American Association of Industrial Nurses) Vol. 15, No. 3.
EYSENCK, H. J. (1953) *Uses and abuses of psychology,* Penguin, London.
EYSENK, H. J. (1966) *Dimensions of personality,* In: Semeonoff B. Personality Assessment. Penguin Modern Psychology Readings.
GALE, R. C. (1972) A hospital occupational health service. *Nursing Times,* March 30th and April 6th.
GARLAND, T. O. (1968) Care of hospital nursing staff. *Nursing Times.* 1968. Vol. 64, No. 7.
HALMOS, P. (1965) *The faith of the counsellors.* Constable, London.
HAMBLIN, D. (1974) *Mental health, self-fulfilment and the philosophy of counselling.* Lecture given at the Royal College of Nursing, London.
HARTE, J. D. (1974) *Occupational health for Area Health Authority Staff.* Proceedings, Royal Society of Health Congress.
HEALTH AND SAFETY COMMISSION (1977) *Occupational health services—the way ahead.* H.M.S.O., London.
HUNT, D. (1975) OH in the National Health Service. *Nursing Mirror,* September 11th.
INTERNATIONAL COMMITTEE ON OCCUPATIONAL MENTAL HEALTH (1970) *Stress in industry.* Proceedings of a Seminar. Dr. J. L. Kearns, Robert Murray Associates, London. (Hogarth Press).
KENNEDY, E. (1977) *On becoming a counsellor—a basic guide for non-professional counsellors.* Gill and Macmillan Ltd., Dublin.

100

KREWSON, K. A. (1971) What is clear to you—is very clear—to you! *Occupational Health Nursing* (American Association of Occupational Health Nursing) Vol. 19, No. 10, p. 20

LOESCH, I. C. AND N. A. (1975) What do you say after you say Mm-hmm? *American Journal of Nursing* 75(5) 807–809.

LLOYD, P. (1975) Development in the U.K. *Nursing Mirror,* September 11th.

MCFARLANE, J. K. (1975) *A charter for caring.* (The Nursing Lecture, 1975) Royal College of Nursing, London.

NASH, P. (1975) Nursing stress. *Nursing Times,* March 20th

OGSTON, D. G. (1970) Counselling students in a hospital school of nursing. *The Canadian Nurse.* April, p. 52–3.

PAYNE, S. L. (1951) *The art of asking questions.* Princeton University Press.

PROOPS, M. (1972) What the reader seeks and what the aunties give. *Royal Society of Health Journal,* Vol. 92, No. 5, p. 250.

RADWANSKI, D. AND PEARSON, J. C. G. (1972) *Occupational Health Nursing in Scotland. Trans. Soc. Occup. Med.* (1972) 22, 122–125.

RAYNER, C. (1972) Plugging the gap. *Royal Society of Health Journal,* Vol. 92, No. 5, pp. 251–254.

REVANS, R. W. (1964) *Standards for morale. Cause and effect in hospitals.* Nuffield Provincial Hospitals Trust.

RODGER, A. (1952) *The seven point plan.* National Institute of Industrial Psychology, London.

ROGERS, C. R. (1965) *Client centered therapy.* Houghton, Mifflin, Boston, Mass. (1942) *Counselling & psychotherapy.* Houghton, Mifflin, Boston, Mass.

ROYAL COLLEGE OF NURSING (1973) *Rcn comment on the report of the Committee on Nursing,* Rcn., London.

SÄYNAJÄRVI, R. (1969) Education of the occupational health nurse in Finland. *Occ. Hlth.,* Vol. XXI, No. 2. (Macmillan Journals Ltd. now Baillière Tindall).

SEMEONOFF, B. (1966) *Personality assessment.* Penguin Modern Psychology Readings.

STANDING CONFERENCE FOR THE ADVANCEMENT OF COUNSELLING. (now British Council for Counselling)
Opportunities and courses in counselling, 1975.
Report: *Counselling: standards and practice,* Consultation No. 2, 1973
Report: *Training for counselling,* consultation No. 3. 1974.
Report: *Counselling in a work setting,* consultation No. 4. 1974.
What is SCAC? What is Counselling? 1974.

SLANEY, B. (Ed.) (1979) *Occupational Health Nursing.* Croom Helm, London.

STEWART, W. (1973) *An introduction to counselling.*
(1978) Nursing and counselling—a conflict of roles? *Occ. Hlth.* Vol. 30, No. 10. (Baillière, Tindall, London)
(1978) *Guide to counselling,* (first of a series, based on handbook, published by Wessex Regional Health Authority) "*Occ Hlth*", Vol. 30, No. 11, et seq. 1978. Vol. 31, No. 1. et seq. (1979) Health services counselling, Pitman Medical London.

TRUAX, C. B. AND CARKHUFF, R. R. (1967) *Towards effective counselling and psychotherapy.* Aldine, Chicago.

TYLER, L. F. (1953) *The work of the counsellor*. Appleton-Century-Crofts Inc., New York.

VENABLES, E. (1973) *Counselling*. National Marriage Guidance Council, London.

WALLIS, J. H. (1974) *Personal counselling*. George Allen & Unwin, London.

WORLD HEALTH ORGANIZATION (1970) *Trends in European Nursing Services*. W.H.O. Regional Office for Europe, Copenhagen.